THE LAST DANCE

SAVING INDIA'S DANCING BEARS

By Alan Knight OBE and Sean Whyte

G2 Entertainment

First edition published in the UK in 2019

Print Edition ISBN 978 1 78281 7000

G2 Entertainment, Unit 16, Beaufort Road, Reigate, Surrey, RH2 9DJ

Design by Alex Young

In memory of

Sir Michael Uren OBE

1923-2019

This book is published in Memory of Sir Michael Uren OBE who was a major donor to IAR over many years and without whom the bear sanctuaries in India and the Orangutan rescue centre in Borneo would have taken so much longer to build.

Alan Knight OBE, Chief Executive, International Animal Rescue (IAR)

Dedicated to

Lisa Milella BVSc Dipl. EVDC MRCVS

I dedicate this book to my dear friend Lisa Milella for whom I have the greatest respect and admiration. She joined our veterinary team to help IAR trustee and dentist Paul Cassar develop a reliable system for treating the teeth of our rescued dancing bears. Lisa's knowledge and enthusiasm have helped to impart skills and produce procedures which have vastly improved the bears' welfare. Lisa and Paul have trained the vets of Wildlife SOS to the very highest standards. Dr Arun Sha, Veterinary Director of Wildlife SOS, recently commented that Lisa had not only improved the knowledge of his veterinary team but had started a veterinary dentistry revolution in the whole of India. There can surely be no higher accolade than that!

Alan Knight OBE, Chief Executive, International Animal Rescue (IAR)

Contents

Chapter 1.

Agra Bear Rescue Facility

Page 10

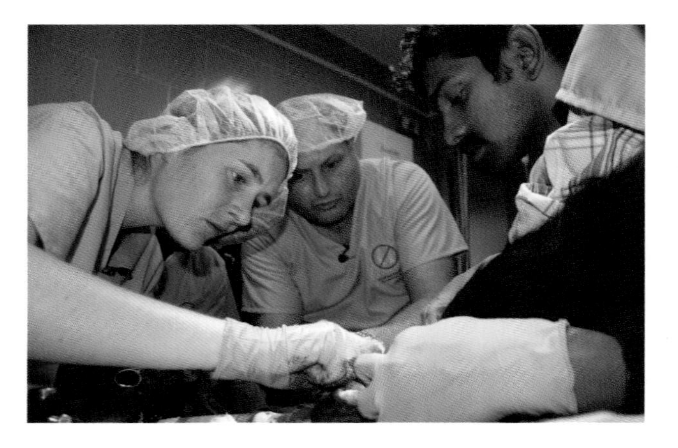

Chapter 2.

Orthodontics

Page 61

Chapter 3.

Enrichment

Page 68

Chapter 4.

Kalandar community

Page 76

Chapter 5.

Bhopal Bear Rescue Facility

Page 84

Chapter 6.

Bannerghatta Bear Rescue Centre

Page 90

Chapter 7.

The last bear rescued

Page 127

Acknowledgements:

Suvidha Bhatnagar, Paul Cassar and the staff of Grange Dental surgery in Chichester, Mary Hutton and Matt Hunt from Free the Bears, The International Animal Rescue teams around the world, The Kalandar community, Lis Key, Lisa Milella, Kartick Satyanarayan, Geeta Seshamani, Sir Michael Uren OBE, the entire team at the Wildlife SOS sanctuaries and offices in India. Janice Bennett and the trustees of the Michael Uren Foundation, Liz Varney, Margaret Whyte.

Photographs:

The authors and publisher would like to thank the following photographers for the free use of their photographs: Roger Allen, Jo Bradford, Martin Gaunt, Gavin Parsons, Wildlife SOS.

Introduction *by Alan Knight OBE*

International Animal Rescue (IAR) has been working in India since 1995 when we first began rescuing and treating stray dogs and cats that were in desperate need of help.

We started off in a rented house where the vets sterilised animals on the kitchen table. However, we soon decided that a permanent rescue centre was needed. We also needed to register the charity in India and deal with the copious documentation required by the Indian Government.

To help us navigate the complex corridors of power that make up the Government of India, we were introduced to Geeta Seshamani who runs Friendicoes SECA – an animal rescue charity based in the centre of New Delhi. Geeta steered us on a steady course and arranged for us to meet Maneka Gandhi who was a minister at the time and responsible for animal welfare. With Maneka's help we purchased a small property, set up a veterinary clinic and erected dog kennels to enable us to continue our work in Goa.

During a visit to Geeta's house in Defence Colony in New Delhi I noticed huge stacks of leaflets describing the plight of the dancing bears in India. I asked Geeta about the project and she explained that she had set up a charity to help India's wildlife called Wildlife SOS (WSOS). Geeta and co-founder Kartick Satyanarayan had identified a total of some 1200 sloth bears in desperate need of rescuing from the streets of India.

It was clear that Wildlife SOS needed help if they were to achieve their goal.

Geeta Seshamani receiving a sloth bear into our Agra facility.

Geeta introduced me to Kartick and together they told me about the plight of the sloth bear. They explained that these bears had been used as dancing bears all over India for more than 300 years.

A nomadic tribe called the Kalandars used bears and other animals to earn a living by entertaining the courts of the Mughal emperors.

Over the centuries the Kalandar tribe had become more and more marginalised from society, both socially and economically. They were forced to become nomadic, travelling long distances with their bears in order to scrape a meagre wage with which to keep their families alive.

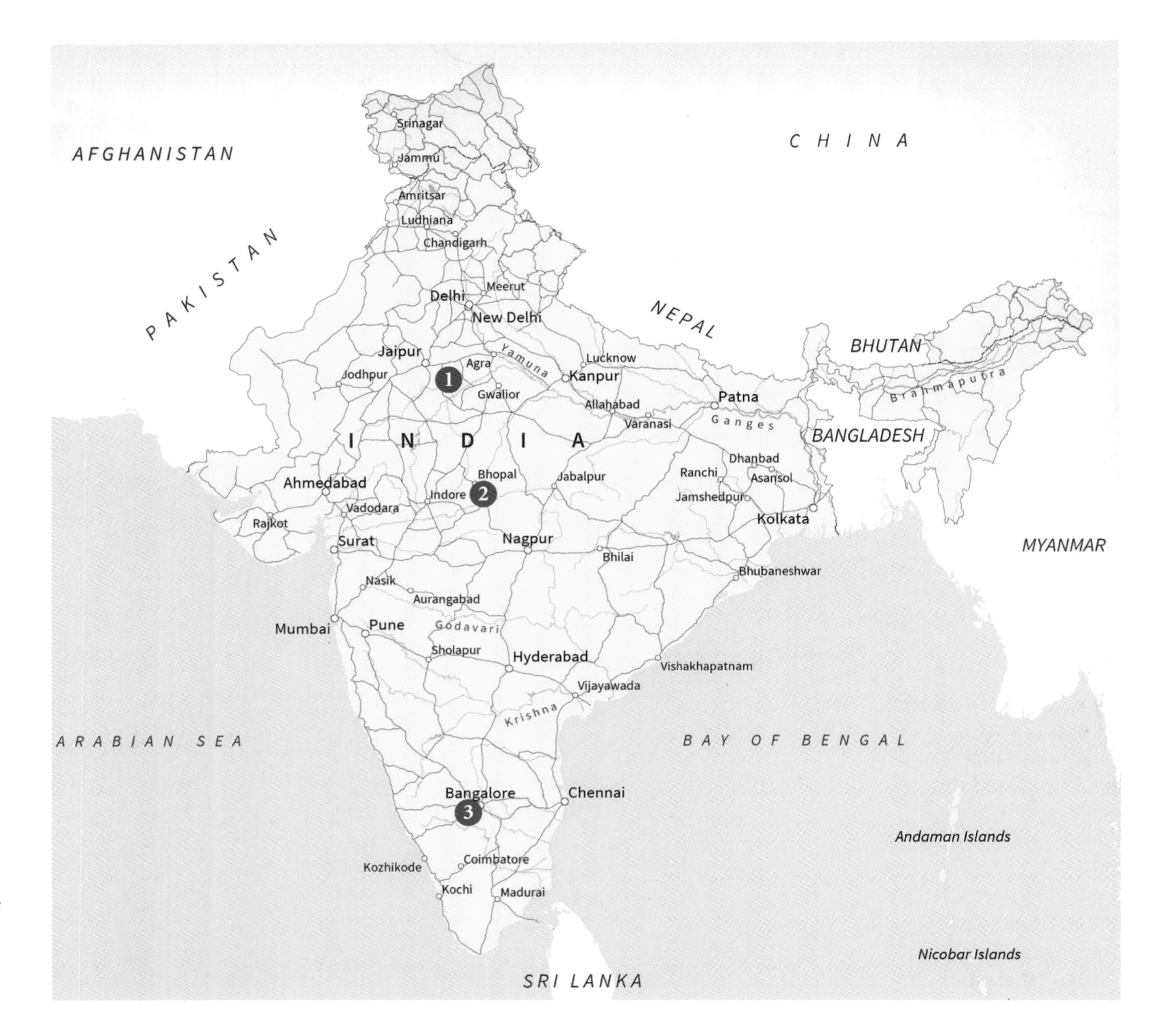

Map of India showing the 3 bear sanctuaries:

❶ Agra Bear Rescue Facility ❷ Bhopal Bear Rescue Facility ❸ Bannerghatta Bear Rescue

The Sloth Bear

Sloth bears *(Melursus ursinus)* have shaggy black coats, pale, short-haired muzzles and long, curved claws which they use to excavate termite and ant colonies. They have a distinctive cream coloured "V" mark on their chests. Sloth bear nostrils are capable of closing to protect the bears from dust or insects when raiding termite or ant nests. They have a gap in their teeth which allows them to suck up insects by making a tube with their lips.

Sloth bears can grow up to five or six feet long. They stand two or three feet high at the shoulder and weigh from 55Kg or 120lbs (female) to 140Kg or 310lbs (male.) They can be found from the far north to the far south of India and Sri Lanka. They also live in southern Nepal and have been reported in Bhutan and Bangladesh. The sloth bear is listed as vulnerable on the World Conservation Union (IUCN) Red List of Threatened Animals and the population trend is classed as decreasing. Sloth bears live in a variety of dry and wet forests and also in some grasslands where boulders and scattered shrubs and trees provide shelter.

When trees are in fruit, sloth bears dine on mango, fig and other fruits, and also on some flowers. However, ants and termites, dug out of their cement-hard mounds, are the year-round staple. Sloth bears are good climbers and will scale trees to knock down honeycombs and eat the sweet honey found inside. They also eat beetles, grubs and other insects to supplement their diet. Sloth bears sometimes come into conflict with humans, particularly in lean times when hunger drives the bears to raid villagers' crops.

Sloth bears mate during the hot season – May, June and July – and females usually give birth to two cubs six to seven months later. Cubs are born in underground dens and stay there for several months.

Sloth bears are normally solitary and most are nocturnal. In protected areas they may be active during the day. If threatened they will stand on their hind legs and use their sizeable claws for protection.

AGRA

The Agra Bear Rescue Facility (ABRF) lies a few kilometres north of the famous Taj Mahal in the north of India. Chosen for the first rescue centre because of its close proximity to the homes of many Kalandar families, it is run by IAR's Indian partners Wildlife SOS and their expert team of vets and keepers. Covering over 400 acres, the facility is situated on land within the government-owned Sur Sarovar Bird Sanctuary, under the overall supervision of the Uttar Pradesh Forestry Department. The sanctuary is the largest sloth bear rescue facility of its kind in the world, providing a beautiful natural forest habitat where over 180 bears roam freely after a period of quarantine and rehabilitation. The socialisation areas have freshwater bathing pools, purpose-built dens, feeding and resting areas, as well as climbing frames and other types of environmental enrichment. The facility first became operational on 18th December 2002 when the first six dancing bears were surrendered at its gates.

The torturous life of a dancing bear always began as a cub. Captured most likely from deep inside a cave while their mother was away finding food, all her terrified cubs would be taken away in sacks, often over long distances with no food or water. This was only the beginning of their lives as slaves to those who went on to torture and starve the bears until they submitted to their captors. It's thought as many as 80% of all cubs stolen and traded died from their wounds or from malnutrition before adulthood.

The sanctuary is fully equipped to treat and rehabilitate rescued bears with a state-of-the-art veterinary surgery allowing accurate diagnosis of injuries and ailments for swift and efficient treatment. As well as suffering from malnutrition and often from diseases such as tuberculosis and leptospirosis, the rescued bears also often need surgery for horrific nose wounds, broken teeth and infected gums.

Building secure homes for over 200 bears was never going to be easy or cheap. The kind and dedicated supporters of IAR and Wildlife SOS made the construction of the Agra Bear Rescue Facility and the two additional facilities in Bangalore and Bhopal possible. Without one kind and caring donor in particular the rescue of so many bears would never have been possible.

Building a future for suffering bears, brick by brick.

As soon as the Agra Bear Rescue Facility was built it was time to provide the bears with some creature comforts. The rescued bears can often be found in a comfy hammock sleeping off a good meal, safe in the knowledge that they no longer have anything to fear.

In 2006 International Animal Rescue and Wildlife SOS signed an agreement on an additional area of land across the Yamuna river to expand the facility to an overall size of about 400 acres of mixed forest and scrubland. More dens were needed, as well as extensive planting of trees and other vegetation to reforest the former farmland. Gradually, a perfect paradise was created where the bears could rest and recover from the trauma of their lives on the streets. A further two rescue centres are located in Bangalore and Bhopal.

Kartick Satyanarayan, co-founder and CEO of IAR partner Wildlife SOS, explains to major donor Sir Michael Uren how his money has been spent and all the good work it has funded.

The first bears to arrive at the Agra facility in December 2002 venture out of their night-time dens to face a new and exciting future. Free from pain and hunger, they have all the time in the world to explore and sniff out ants and termites in their spacious enclosure.

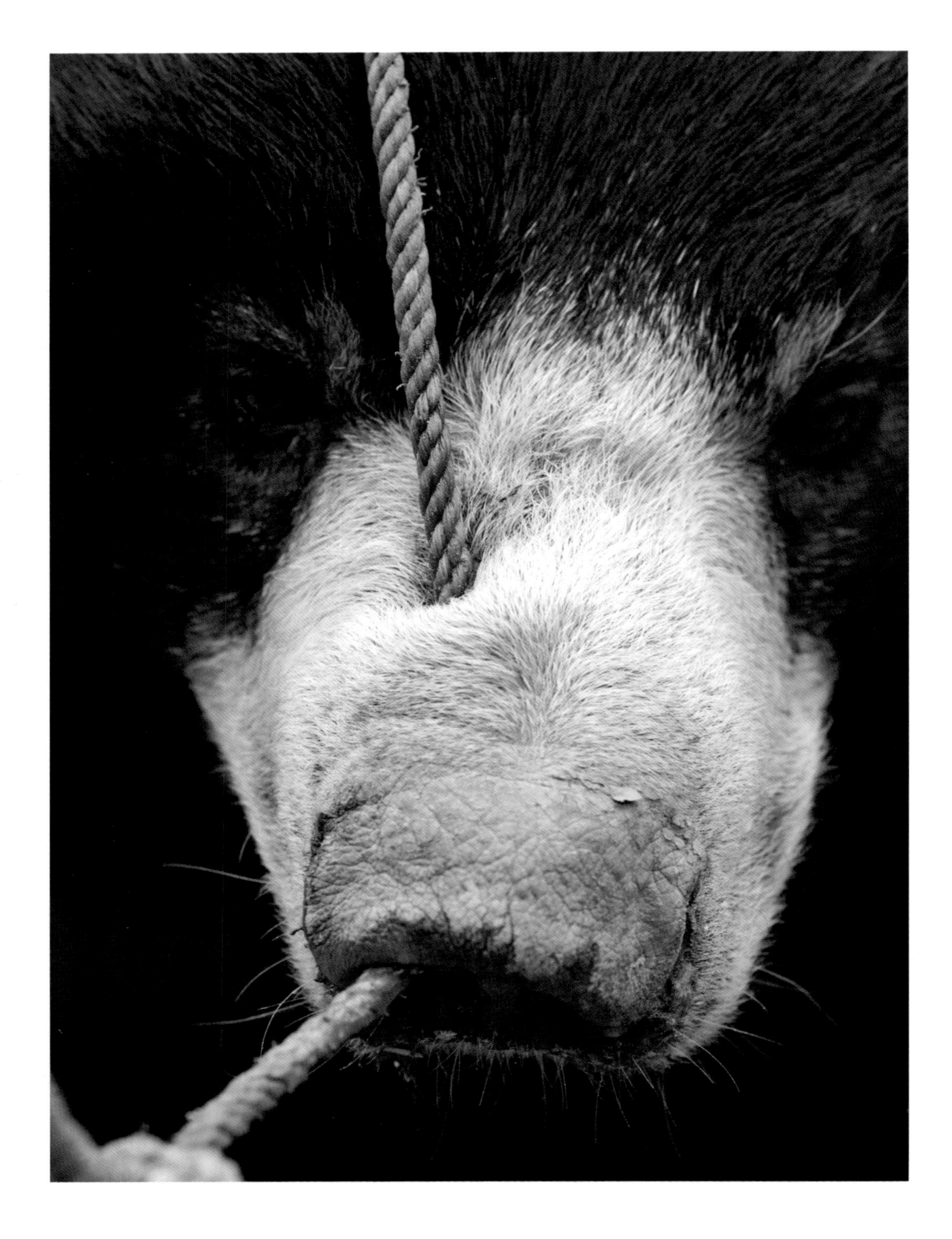

This image illustrates why there was such an urgent need to save the dancing bears. Before they were rescued, they knew only a life of abuse and neglect. They would be forced to work for up to twelve hours a day while suffering unimaginable pain. Thankfully, that is behind them now and they can live out the rest of their lives without ever being harmed or hungry again.

To enable discipline and training to begin, when cubs were about a year old several Kalandar tribespeople would hold a squealing cub down and brutally force a red hot rod some 6.5 inches in length that has been heated over a coal fire through the top of the bears nose and out through the mouth. No anaesthesia or medication was used. A thick rope was then inserted to give the owner total control of the bear – for the rest of the poor animal's life. After four months and before the invariably infected agonising first wound had healed, to enable a thicker rope to be inserted, a second nose piercing was undertaken, this time with the rope pulled out through either nostril.

The rope was attached to the handler's wooden stick which had a piece of metal nailed on the end. When the stick was tapped on the ground and the rope was jerked upwards the bear would stand on its hind legs and appear to dance. The wounds in the bear's nose were never allowed to heal to keep the bear in pain and make it respond to its master's commands.

Tourists would throw money in reaction to what they thought was a bear dancing of its own free will, when in fact the poor creature was attempting to avoid punishment and even more excruciating agony.

Spotlight on BEAN

Bean is as adorable as he is mischievous and that allows him to get away with almost anything. It has been six years since Bean and his sister Bintha were rescued in 2013. They had come to us as terrified orphaned cubs in excruciating pain because their tender muzzles had been mercilessly pierced and their milk teeth broken. To see them at this tender age in so much pain broke our hearts completely. It is impossible to imagine the agony they must have gone through. But now they were safe with us, never again to be touched by the slightest shadow of brutality, exploitation and fear.

After an initial period of justified distrust of human beings and the trauma of being ill-treated, Bean and Bintha gradually began to settle down in their new home. Our veterinarians and bear keepers worked ceaselessly with unparalleled devotion and care and the little bear siblings began to realize that all we have for them is boundless love. Fear gave way to trust and they began to bond with their keepers. Because of their natural attachment with each other, we decided to keep them in the same enclosure so that they could always be together. Bean loves his sister dearly and, peculiarly, he tends to behave like the younger sibling, following Bintha around and imitating her activities. Bintha also behaves like a big sister and is very protective of Bean.

To say that Bean is naughty would be an understatement! Bean is always up to something and there is never a dull moment with him. His keepers, Mathura and Veeru have to be on their toes constantly to make sure he doesn't get himself into trouble. However, since the summer afternoons tend to be very hot in Agra, these are the only few hours when one can catch him resting for a while or splashing about in the pool.

In 2016, the brother and sister were joined by Elvis, another playful cub, and Bean was simply overjoyed. Over time Bean and Elvis have formed a very close and endearing friendship and, together with Bintha, they make a crazy and energetic trio who are always up to some mischief. Among the three of them, Bean loves food the most and can never contain his excitement during his mealtimes. His keeper Veeru says:

"He acts very funny during his mealtimes and is a sight to watch. He can hardly wait for me to come to him with his bowl of porridge. Mangoes and watermelons are his favourite. He also has this very strange habit of gulping down an entire bowl of water after his meals. None of the other bears do it. But I love him dearly. He is easily one of my favourite bears at the centre."

Wildlife SOS

Searching for insects is a bear's favourite pastime.

"The bears need a lot of veterinary treatment when they first arrive at a rescue centre. Most of them suffer from tuberculosis caught from their human handlers. Some are blind as a result of injuries sustained to their eyes when their owners pierced their noses. By far the worst were the mouth and nose injuries often requiring treatment from highly specialised volunteer vets from England. We have even found some bears with maggots in their muzzles."

Dr Yaduraj Khadpekar, Veterinarian, Wildlife SOS

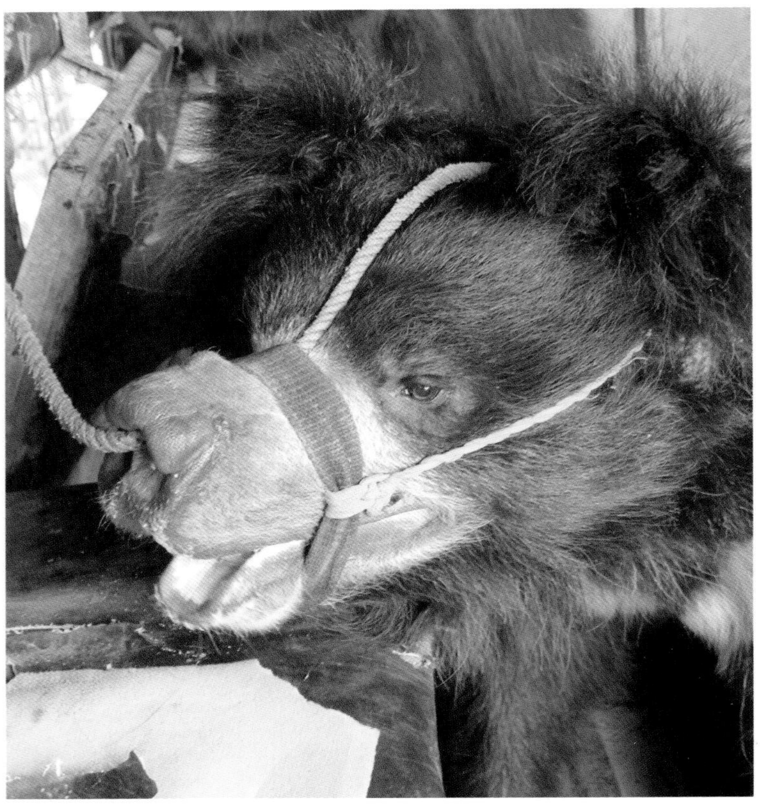

Very sadly, these two bears lost their sight as a result of injuries sustained when their muzzles were pierced.

If it was not for the intervention of International Animal Rescue and its partners to this day this little bear cub would have suffered unimaginable cruelty and hardship as a dancing bear.
(see opposite)

A heart-breaking sight now consigned to history in India.

During the heat of the day some bears like to socialise and share shelter from the sun.

The best of friends.

The bears always have access to water to enjoy a cool dip.

"Dancing bears in India suffered unimaginable cruelty until International Animal Rescue and Wildlife SOS stepped in and set about bringing it to an end. And end it they did! What a huge relief to know that this barbaric practice has been eradicated and bears no longer suffer pain and starvation on the streets of India."

Peter Egan

Actor and animal welfarist Peter Egan is a patron of International Animal Rescue and an active and outspoken campaigner for an end to animal cruelty all around the world.

Spotlight on PEANUT

Peanut was rescued on 21st March 2010 from what would have been an abysmal fate. After going through the trauma of losing his mother, he and three other cubs were about to be smuggled out of India into Nepal. Fortunately, Peanut was received in a relatively healthy condition, which could not be said for some of the other cubs in the group.

Considering the terrible ordeal that Peanut and his brothers had been subjected to, it was no surprise that he reached the Agra Bear Rescue Facility in an anxious state. He initially showed reservations towards the bear keepers and the vets, but eventually grew a close bond to his keeper who put in the work and exhibited the patience that eventually allowed him to gain the little cub's trust. Now, nine years later, he is the only person to whom Peanut has been able to form an attachment. Sadly, although he and his keeper get along immensely well, he still has trouble connecting with the majority of the other bears and humans, which unfortunately results in displays of unpredictable behaviour.

During Peanut's rehabilitation time the team noticed his incredibly voracious appetite. When he first arrived at the centre, he weighed a measly 5.7 kilograms. After being provided with a healthy and consistent diet and first-class care from our vets, he has been able to grow to an impressive 102 kilograms! Over time his tastes have developed, and he currently enjoys chomping on watermelons and slurping up his porridge.

When Peanut is not eating or interacting with his keeper, he can be found relaxing with his brother Pat. Their bond was forged from the moment they were born, which explains why it is so strong. In addition to spending time with Pat, Peanut loves lounging in the pool during hot summer days or playing around with the various structural enrichments that are provided.

Peanut has come a long way since his rescue and he continues to progress here at the Agra Bear Rescue Facility. It is amazing to witness these animals enjoying fulfilling lives, when their fate could have been such a terrible one.

Wildlife SOS

Peanut, always on the hunt for food!

Peanut with Pat, his best friend and brother.

Peanut loves lounging in the pool.

Keeper Gopal Singh with Peanut. This close human contact was only possible in the early post-rescue days and whilst Peanut was adjusting to his new life and making friends with other bears.

Keeper Shrikantha plays with the bear cubs. At first the rescued bears sought out human company - the only kind they had ever known - but they soon reverted to their natural behaviours and human contact stopped.

Comedian and musician Bill Bailey paid a visit to the Agra Bear Rescue Facility in November 2005 and was particularly impressed by the way the project was helping both bears and people.

"What I found fascinating, almost humbling in a way, is the fact that these bears have been treated with an incredible amount of cruelty at the hands of humans and yet here, at the bear sanctuaries, after a comparatively short amount of time, they don't seem to bear a grudge."

"We went to the Kalandar village today and you see how these people rely on the bears for their income. So any solution to the problem has to include them."

Bill Bailey, November 2005

An ardent animal lover, Bill Bailey was deeply moved by the sight of this bear.

The Flood of 2011

In 2010 monsoon rains in India caused a life-threatening situation at the Agra Bear Rescue Facility (ABRF). Rapidly rising floodwaters from the Yamuna River rose almost to the rooftops of some buildings in the sanctuary. The Wildlife SOS team who manage the centre reacted swiftly, moving bears and supplies to dry land by boat and, thanks to their prompt action, no human or animal lives were lost. However, considerable damage was done to the sanctuary, with valuable veterinary equipment ruined and buildings submerged in water and silt. The clean-up operation was time consuming and costly.

A similar situation arose the following year, causing the 70 vets and bear keepers to maintain a round-the-clock vigil to keep the floodwaters at bay. Once again, the team was forced to evacuate the bears from their enclosures and move them to higher ground to keep them safe.

Reporting from the Agra sanctuary, Geeta Seshamani, Co-Founder of Wildlife SOS, said: "*The floodwaters are rising really fast and we are all quite jumpy. All the bears have been moved to safety on higher ground and to enclosures that are above the danger level, but if the floodwaters rise any further, this will lead to major problems. We simply have to find a permanent solution to what is clearly going to be a serious and recurring problem – and that is going to require the construction of new dens and enclosures outside the danger zone. And that means more money on top of what we already need to feed the bears. I just hope we can count on the public and on our supporters to keep us afloat!*"

Flooding only became a problem at the ABRF following the Commonwealth Games in Delhi in October 2010 when the Games village was built on the flood plains of the Yamuna. After the building work for the Games was completed, the management of the flow of the Yamuna River appears to have been altered to prevent the athletes' Games Village from flooding. The knock-on impact of this was felt downstream where, following heavy monsoon rains, floodgates on the river were opened and serious flooding occurred.

The flooded entrance to the Agra Bear Rescue Facility and the submerged billboards and fencing.

The Yamuna River runs on the periphery of the Sur Sarovar Sanctuary where the Agra sanctuary is located and consequently a large portion of this was exposed to serious levels of floodwater.

Alan Knight, Chief Executive of International Animal Rescue, said at the time: *"The alterations to the flow of the river were beyond the control of our partners at Wildlife SOS. We are committed to helping them care for the bears and are calling on our supporters and members of the public to help us provide a long-term solution to this crisis. The thought of losing any of our keepers or any of the bears in the floods is too awful to contemplate and I know the team at Wildlife SOS will do everything they can to ensure this doesn't happen."*

In the years that followed, thankfully, IAR was able to raise extra funds to cover the cost of building additional enclosures and dens on land outside the danger zone to keep bears and people safe from future floods.

Taking food supplies to the bears by boat.

Food for the evacuated bears.

Evacuated bears, safely on dry land and waiting to be fed.

The bears' flooded enclosures.

The Agra Bear Rescue Facility is divided by the Yamuna river seen here in the dry season.

Spotlight on SARASU

Sarasu had spent almost three years tied to the end of a small rope, performing for her master out of fear and pain.

Her Kalandar master would drag her from village to village and force her to make dance-like movements for entertaining both children and adults alike. Things took a different turn for Sarasu when we rescued her from the northern state of Uttar Pradesh in 2005, liberating her from her dreadful life. She was thin, malnourished and weighed just 60 kilograms, when she first arrived at the Agra Bear Rescue Facility.

The emotional trauma that each of these bears goes through is extreme. The nightmare of being mistreated and abused everyday takes a heavy toll on their physical and psychological condition. Sarasu would initially sit quietly in the corner of her quarantine enclosure, presumably waiting for someone to strike at her or drag her through the streets to perform, unaware of the fact that her days of being a dancing bear had finally come to an end.

Given her poor physical condition, the veterinarians immediately prescribed a nutrient enriched diet along with multivitamin supplements and provided her with the love and care that she truly deserved. Over time Sarasu realised that she was in the safe caring hands of our staff who only wished for her steady recovery.

Today, she is a little over seventeen years old and weighs a healthy 124 kilograms. Even though she has grown out of her initial withdrawn state, Sarasu remains a docile and quiet bear who usually keeps to herself. Her favourite place in the enclosure is her den and she rarely wanders beyond a few feet from her home. She is comfortable with her keeper Deena Nath but will run inside her den whenever anyone else tries to approach her.

For the most part Sarasu prefers the solitary life but she did share a special bond with a male bear named Herbie. Sadly, Herbie passed away shortly after being diagnosed with tuberculosis. For a while Sarasu withdrew into herself and was listless and disconnected from everyone, but it's encouraging to see that she is now slowly bonding with another female bear named Pembroke Girl and a male bear named Abhay.

Abhay and Sarasu often play together and they have taken a great liking to our newly designed enrichment - the hanging braid feeders! Sarasu also enjoys climbing trees and foraging. As the trees provide respite from the harsh sun during summers, she spends most of the day resting on the branches or under their shade. She is one of the few bears that dislikes multigrain porridge and will only drink milk and munch on fruits. Watermelons, mangoes and grapes are her absolute favourite during the summer season.

Wildlife SOS

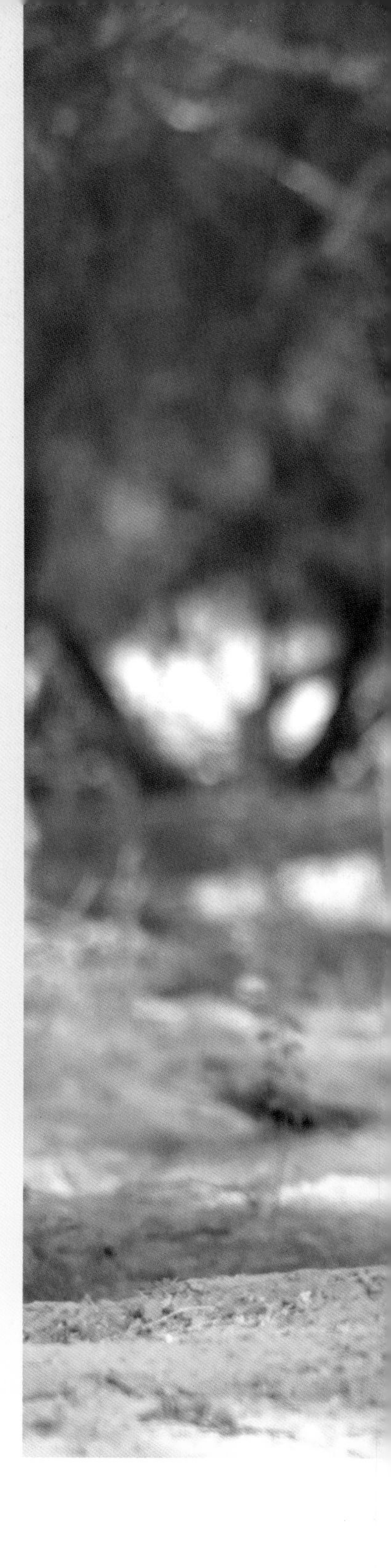

Sarasu's muzzle is scarred from her days as a 'dancing bear'.

Sarasu (and Abhay, below) extracting food from a hanging braid feeder which encourages the bears to look and work for food.

Sarasu (L) and Abhay (R).

Some of the hundreds of young trees planted to preserve and replenish the natural forest habitat at the Agra Bear Rescue Facility.

Exploring their vast enclosures is something all the bears enjoying doing.

Happy, contented bears, free from the pain and disfigurement of metal rings or coarse ropes in their noses. 90% of the bears rescued had had their canine teeth forcibly removed by their handlers at between the ages of eight to ten months. and 80% were missing their incisor teeth. Teeth are extracted by using an iron rod and wooden hammer to dislodge them by force; this is done without anaesthesia or medication.

The bears are free to do as they please in their enclosures.

Now enjoying life at the Agra Bear Rescue Facility.

The bears' scars are a lasting reminder of the abuse they have suffered.

Whatever the dish of the day was, this bear was in no mood for sharing!

Information panels at the Agra Bear Rescue Facility.

Prior to being rescued the bears were kept tethered on the dusty roadside and never had a chance to enjoy their natural habitat.

Super-size bear paws come in handy as sun-shades!

A sloth bear's claws are perfectly designed for digging and breaking open rock-hard termite nests. Sadly, in captivity bear owners would cut the nails twice a year using a nut-cracker, partly to enable the bear to walk on roads, but nails would also be sold by some to supplement their income with the demand coming from both local and foreign buyers. If a buyer wanted a full-length nail then one would be pulled out in its entirety, causing the bear unimaginable pain.

Spotlight on POLLY

Rescued in 2008 at the age of six from West Bengal, former dancing bear Polly was in a heart-wrenching state when she first set foot into the Agra Bear Rescue Facility. She was weak, half-starved and in absolute agony from a muzzle infection. It had been caused by the constant tugging of a coarse rope threaded through an open wound in her delicate muzzle. The history of psychological and physical mistreatment was evident from Polly's aversion to humans, coupled with the stereotypical behaviour she exhibited, such as head bobbing and pacing.

The first step on her road to recovery was to finally liberate Polly from the coarse rope that had for years caused her excruciating pain. Her infected muzzle was attended to with great care and we made every effort to gradually gain her trust and acceptance. With time and proper care, we were able to help her overcome the atrocities of her past and have watched her grow stronger and healthier every day. Now seventeen years old and weighing approximately 86 kilos, this playful resident of Agra Bear Rescue Facility is almost unrecognisable! Her muzzle has healed completely, leaving behind only a scar, and her temperament has seen a positive transition from utter distrust of humans to a more lenient behaviour with her keepers.

Polly is easily one of the most amicable bears at the centre and she revels in the company of her closest bear buddies Brabu and Suraj. She loves eating all kinds of seasonal fruits and wolfs down bowls of honey-laced porridge, making sure to lick her bowl completely clean after every meal. Polly is extremely fond of climbing trees, playing with honey log enrichments and munching on coconuts. During the hot summer months, one can see her running around in the field, following the water sprinklers and splashing about in the pool.

Thanks to all the love and attention she has received since being rescued, Polly has been saved not only physically but emotionally too.

Wildlife SOS

Polly anticipating a tasty treat of honey.

Polly playing happily with a honey covered log.

Choosing a comfy spot to bask in the sun on the climbing frame.

"I'm proud to have been involved in the dancing bear rescue project which has given hundreds of rescued bears a peaceful, pain-free retirement in sanctuaries in India. After years of abuse and neglect, they are treated with compassion and respect and their former handlers have been found new, humane ways to earn a living. IAR and its coalition partners found a solution that helped both animals and people and so were able to end a practice that had caused immense suffering to countless captive bears over hundreds of years. What a monumental achievement!"

Scott Miller BVSc, MRCVS

Vet and broadcaster Scott Miller visited the Bannerghatta Bear Rescue Centre in 2007 to see the project for himself. He has since become a patron and staunch supporter of the work of International Animal Rescue.

AGRA BEAR RESCUE FACILITY

BEAR STATUS

WILDLIFE SOS

MONTH YEAR

ENCL	MALE	FEMALE	TOTAL
1	6	4	10
2	-	8	8
3	8	10	18
4	1	4	5
5	1	-	1
6	1	4	5
7	5	3	8
8	10	7	17
9	6	8	14
10	19	7	26
11	9	15	24
12	9	7	16
13	13	14	27
14	18	10	28
15	1	-	1
16	2	1	3
QUARANTINE			
TOTAL	109	102	211

ENC 1 AND 2	ENC 3	ENC 4	ENC 5, 6 AND 7	ENC 8
		FEMALE		
ADELAIDE	KANMANI	KAJOL	GOPI	UMA
AISHWARYA	BIJILI	MADHU	KIRTI	SUND
CHAMELI	MANGEE	MAHARANI	SONA	RADH
DEEPIKA	BUTTERBALL	SONALI	PEMBROKE GIRL	PINCH
GAIL	CHAMPA		SARASU	MADI
PRIYA	RANI		SHAMATHA	MAYRE
JOTHIKA	TARINI		LUFE	NANDHI
JULEE	BINTHA			
KAVERI	MANALI			
SHALINI	POOJA			
MAHESWARI				
PINKY				
		MALE		
NISHANT	CHOTU	JONNY	HERBIE	AKKI
GOLDIE	SHYAMU		NIPO	RAM
MICHEL	KABILAN		RANJAN	RENGU
ROCKY	VISHNU		AMAL	ROSHAN
RAJIV	BEAN		ABHAY	BOBBY
GANESHA	DAMRU		LALOO MASTER	BRA[illegible]U
	AMITABH		AKBAR	SURAJ
	BHOOPSINGH			THARUN
				VARUN
				GUJRAL

Charts listing numbers and names of the 211 bears in the Agra Bear Rescue Facility at that time. Detailed records are kept of all the bears and their health monitored daily.

Educating the public about the bears and the work done to rescue and care for them is vitally important.

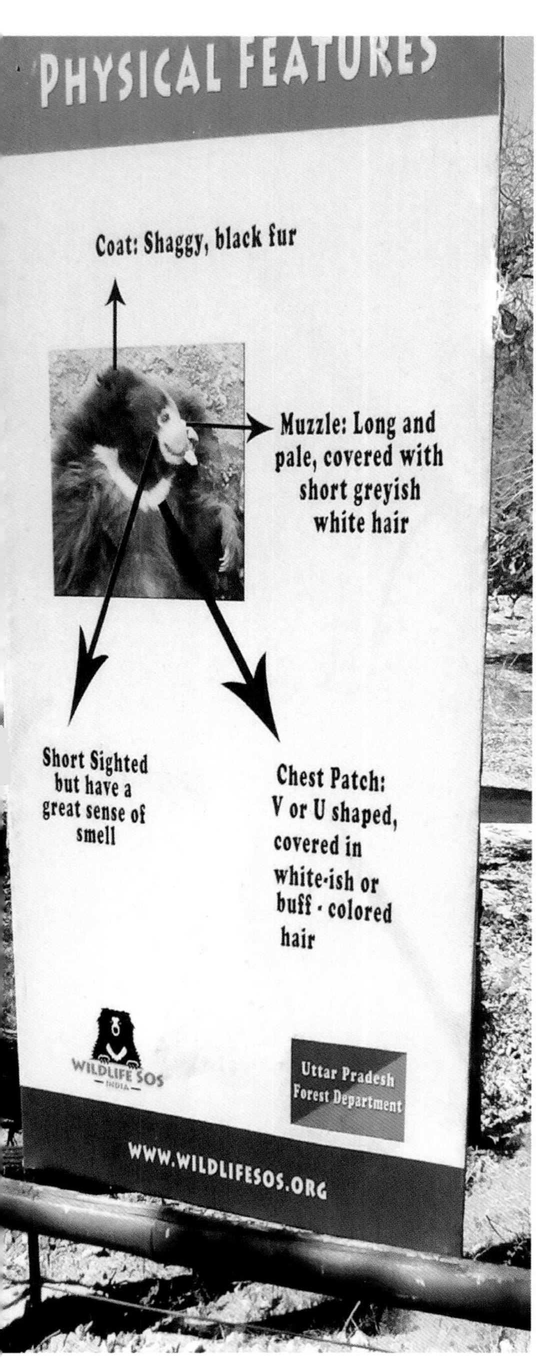
PHYSICAL FEATURES
Coat: Shaggy, black fur
Muzzle: Long and pale, covered with short greyish white hair
Short Sighted but have a great sense of smell
Chest Patch: V or U shaped, covered in white-ish or buff - colored hair
WILDLIFE SOS
INDIA
Uttar Pradesh Forest Department
WWW.WILDLIFESOS.ORG

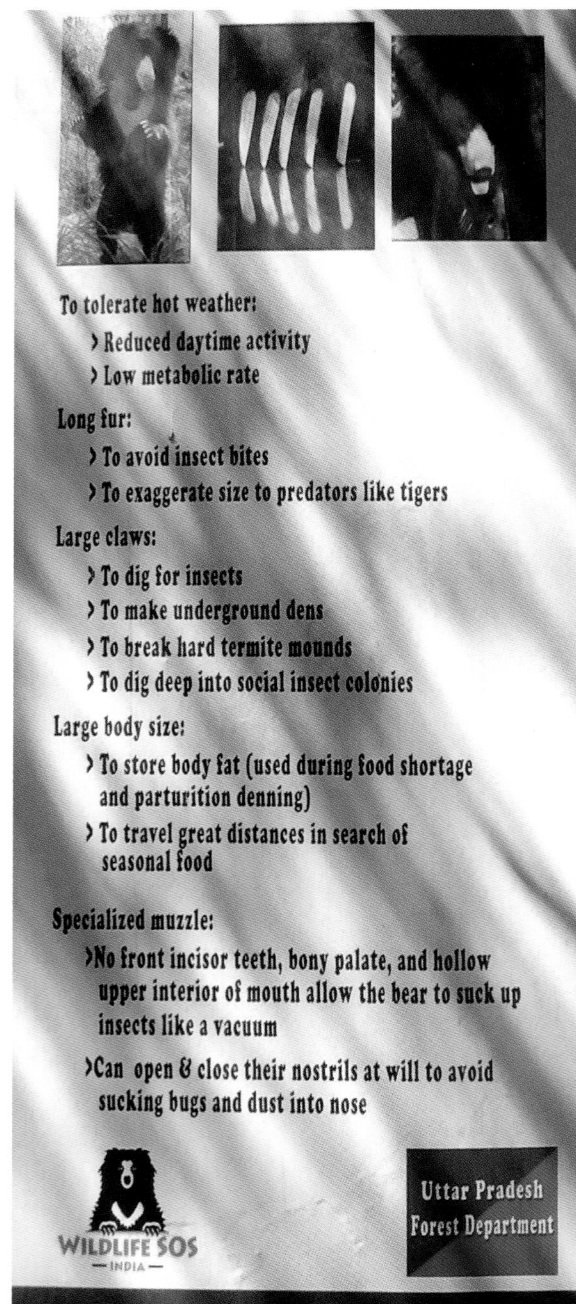
To tolerate hot weather:
› Reduced daytime activity
› Low metabolic rate
Long fur:
› To avoid insect bites
› To exaggerate size to predators like tigers
Large claws:
› To dig for insects
› To make underground dens
› To break hard termite mounds
› To dig deep into social insect colonies
Large body size:
› To store body fat (used during food shortage and parturition denning)
› To travel great distances in search of seasonal food
Specialized muzzle:
›No front incisor teeth, bony palate, and hollow upper interior of mouth allow the bear to suck up insects like a vacuum
›Can open & close their nostrils at will to avoid sucking bugs and dust into nose
WILDLIFE SOS
INDIA
Uttar Pradesh Forest Department

DIET
Slothbears are insectivore.
This means that they eat mostly insects, like ants and termites.
The bears also eat sugar rich fruits and flowers, and they LOVE honey!
Please sponsor a bottle of honey or some fruit for your favorite bear!
WILDLIFE SOS
INDIA
Uttar Pradesh Forest Department
WWW.WILDLIFESOS.ORG

Orthodontics (Bear Dentistry)

by Lisa Milella BVSc, European Veterinary Specialist in Dentistry

When each bear was rescued and brought to the sanctuary he or she would undergo a complete health examination. During one of these examinations Alan Knight photographed the mouth of Jo, a dancing bear rescued from Bondla zoo. The image showed how all four canine teeth had deliberately been smashed by the Kalandar nomads. He showed the photo to Paul Cassar, a trustee of IAR, who is also a dentist, confirming that these bears desperately needed dental treatment. Broken teeth like this are not only extremely painful because the nerve becomes exposed, they also frequently become infected, often resulting in tooth root abscesses. These bears were living with chronic continuous pain, pain that would have us see an emergency dentist on a Bank Holiday. Not knowing much about animal dentistry, Paul googled "veterinary dentist" and found me, and I was only too willing to help with the project.

It took us a year to organise the first trip to the Agra Bear Rescue Facility and arrange all the necessary equipment.

Under general anaesthetic, we examined each mouth and took x-rays of the affected teeth. This helped us decide whether the tooth could be treated by performing root canal treatment or whether it needed to be extracted. Extraction is a more traumatic procedure for the bear as the root of the tooth is about 7cm long and 2cm wide, embedded deep in the jaw bone. The gum needed to be surgically lifted away from the bone and some bone removed before the root was loosened and extracted. The gum was then replaced and the holes stitched closed to prevent food getting impacted in the extraction sites. This technique only allows one tooth to be treated at a time, whereas two or more teeth could be treated simultaneously if root canal treatment was performed. Root canal treatment was also more challenging compared to humans or dogs and cats because of the size of the tooth and the degree of infection. The procedures would last at least 3-4 hours as there was so much damage and infection in each bear's mouth. We also found other dental problems requiring treatment, the most serious, and unfortunately in a number of bears, was the presence of oral cancerous lumps, most likely as the result of the years of continuous inflammation and infection in the bears' mouths. These lumps interfered with their eating and, once removed, dramatically improved the bears' quality of life.

An essential part of the dentistry project was to train the sanctuary vets to carry out this much- needed dentistry. Over the years Paul and I have treated nearly 150 bears – and over a thousand teeth - but most importantly we have transferred our skills to an outstanding group of sanctuary vets who are now more than capable of treating the bears themselves.

Dr Lisa Milella BVSc Dip EVDC MRCVS

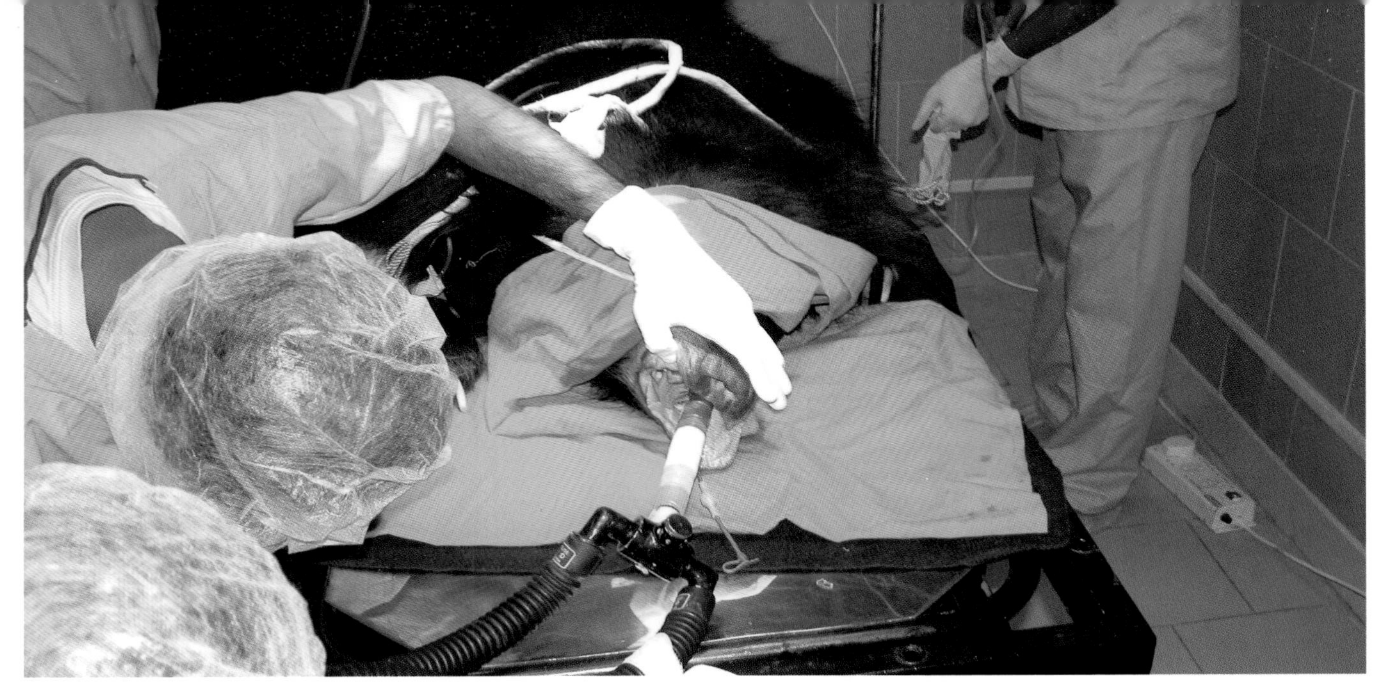

Being prepared for dental treatment.

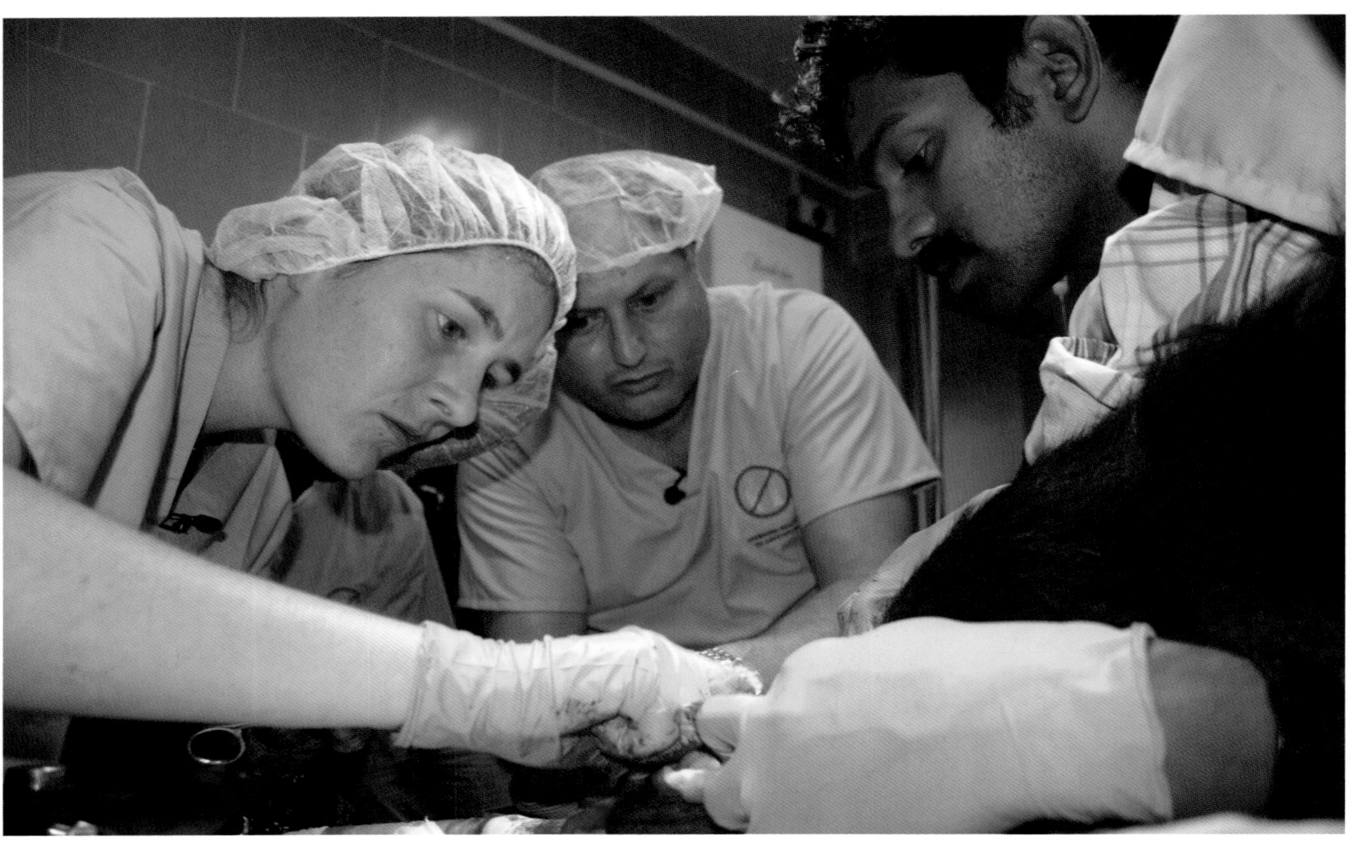

Lisa Milella, Paul Cassar and Dr Arun Sha of Wildlife SOS examine the teeth of an anaesthetised bear.

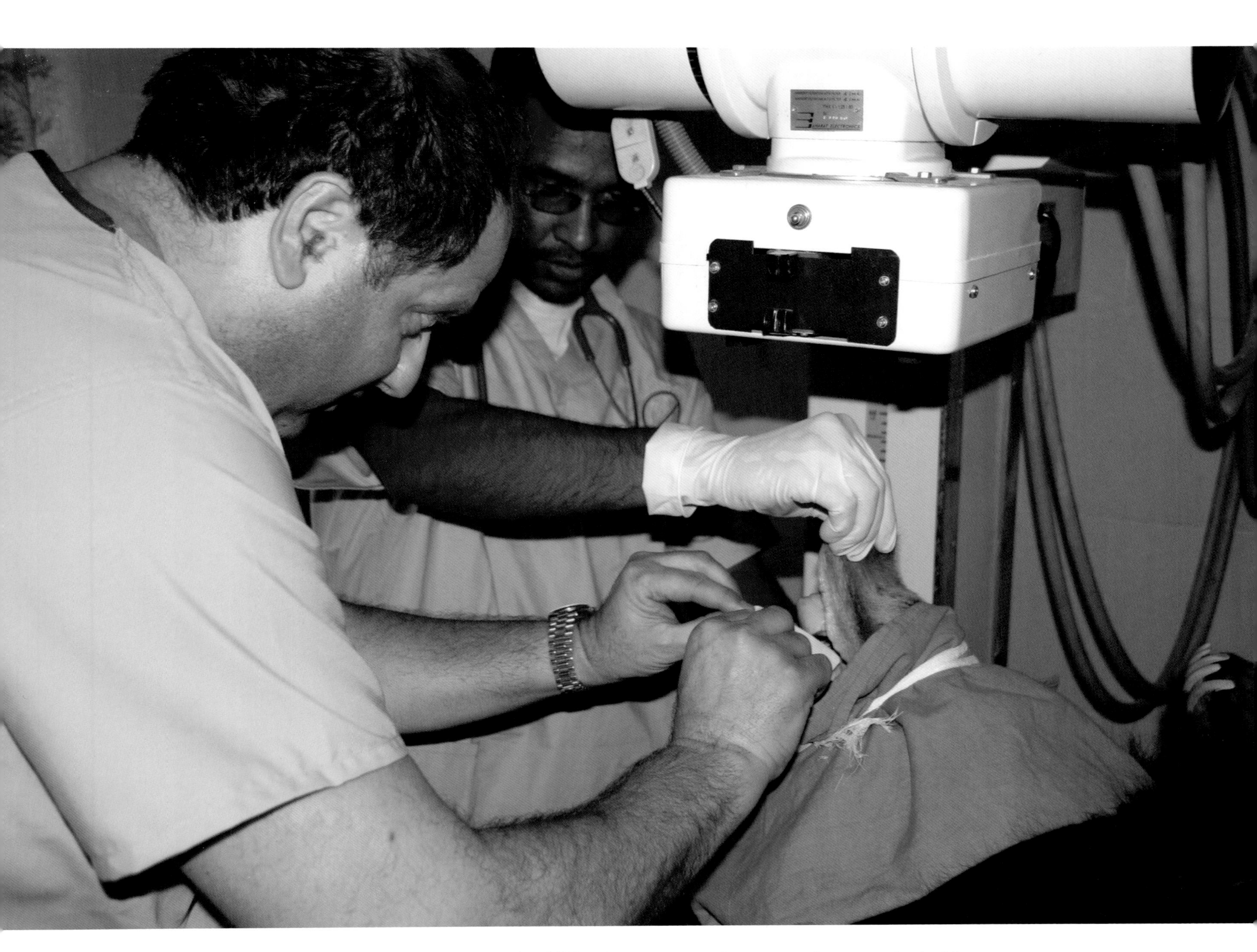

Paul Cassar and Dr Ilayaraja of Wildlife SOS prepare to take an xray of an anaesthetised bear.

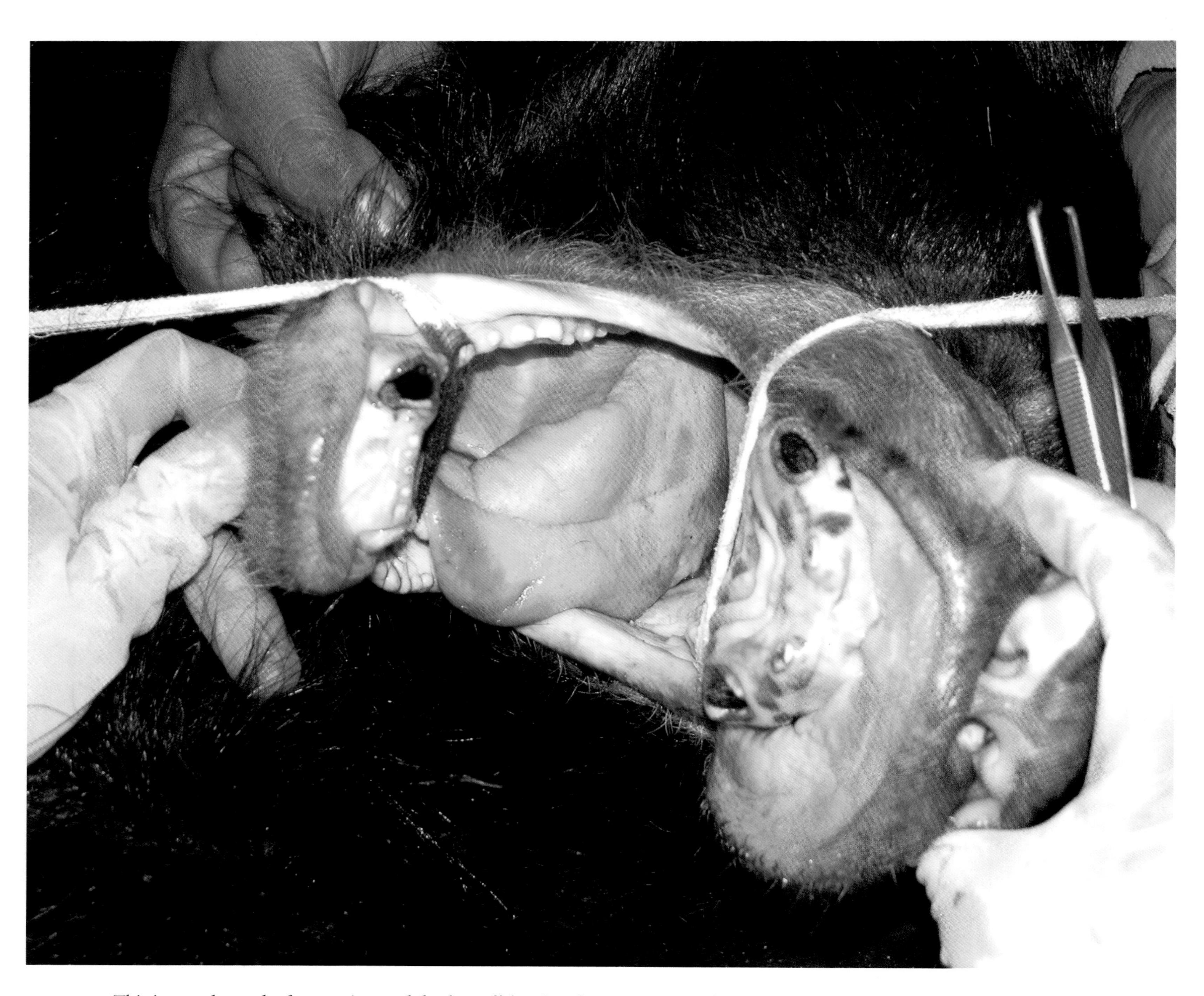

This image shows the four canine teeth broken off, leaving the nerves exposed. The red areas around the teeth show infection.

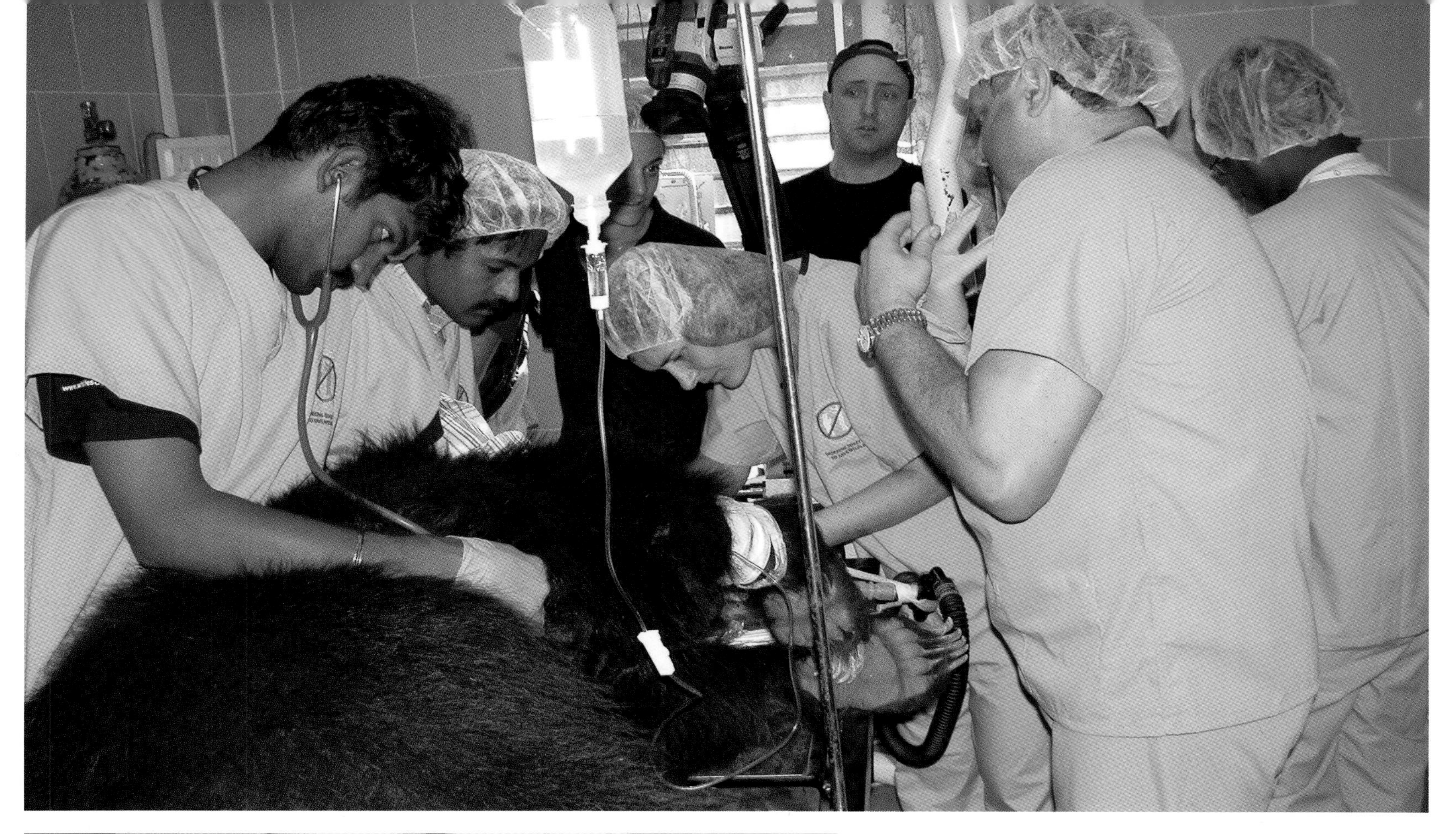

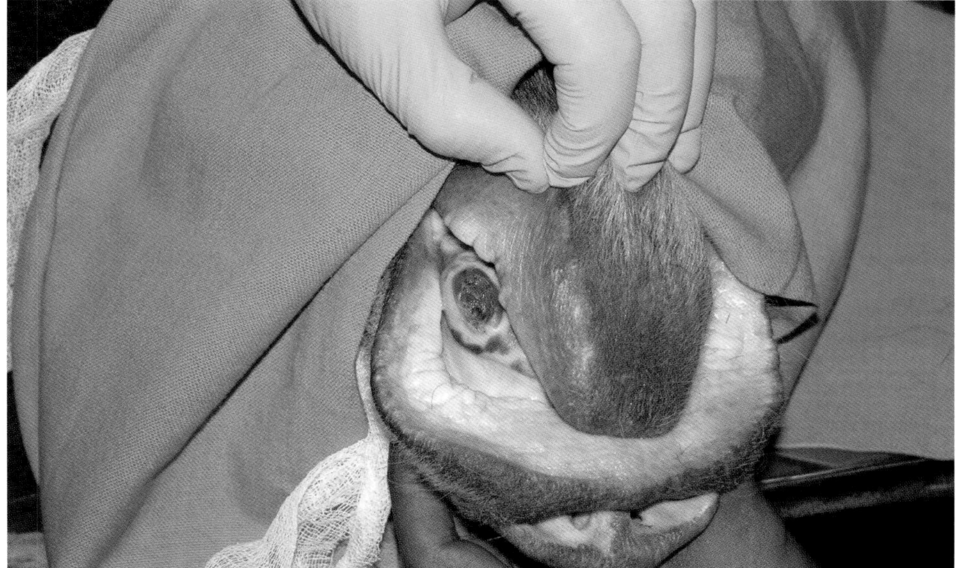

The condition of the anaesthetised bears is monitored closely during dental surgery.

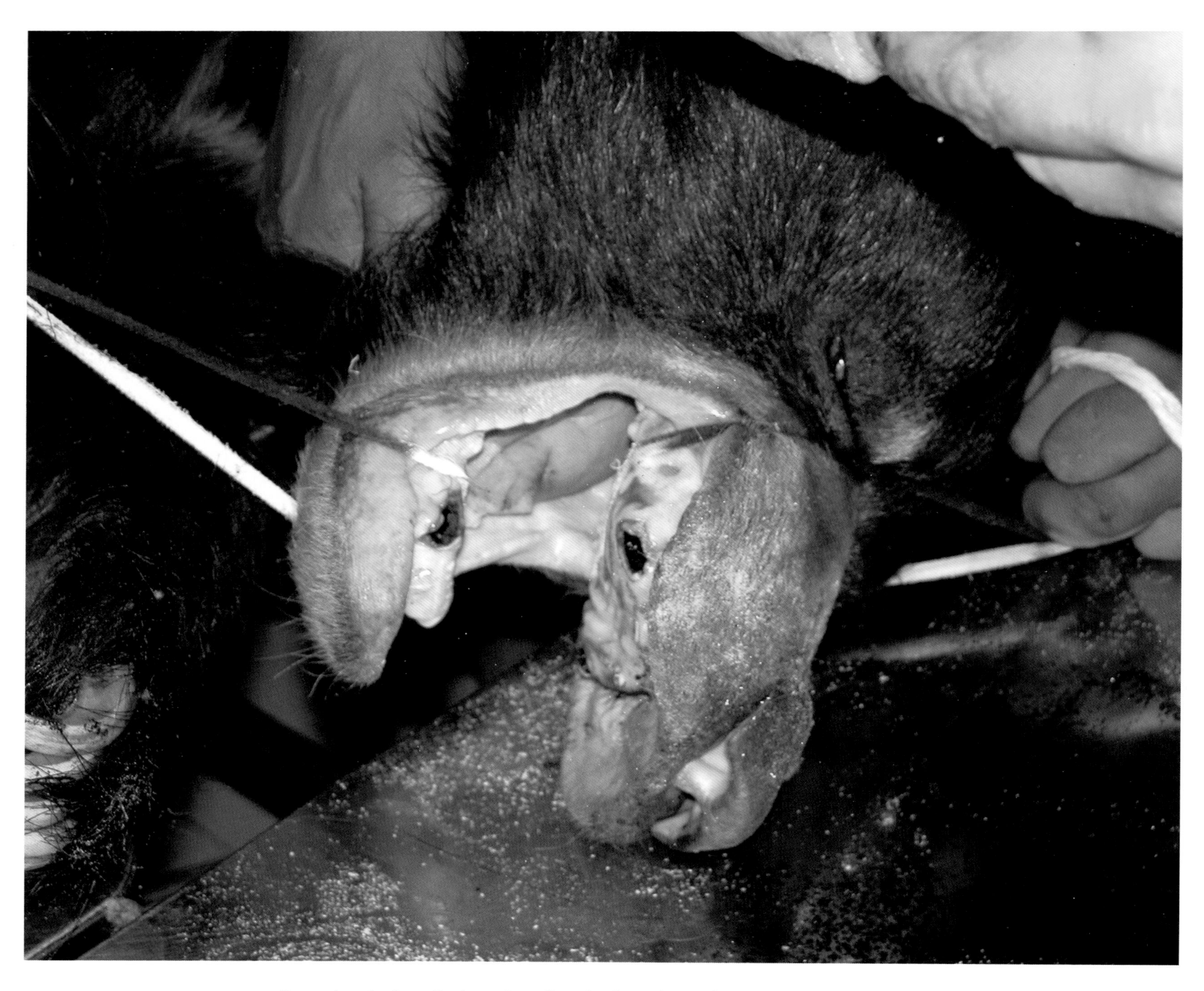

Preparing the bear for insertion of a tube down its trachea prior to dental surgery.

"Back in 2005, our discovery of the shocking state of the dancing bears' teeth came as a complete revelation to us all. Although the rescued bears were no longer being abused and starved on the streets of India, many of them were still in agony from broken teeth and infected gums. Our mission was to relieve their suffering and repair the damage so that the bears could live pain-free for the rest of their lives.

Under Lisa Milella's leadership, the project has pioneered exciting new techniques for tackling dental problems in all kinds of exotic wildlife. The importance of good dental health to an animal's wellbeing is still not recognised in many parts of the world and our work can play a vital role in training and educating vets and animal carers in this crucial area of animal welfare.

I couldn't be more proud to be part of this ground-breaking project which has already transformed the lives of so many suffering animals and promises to continue to do so for years to come."

Paul Cassar, dentist and Trustee of International Animal Rescue

Enrichment

The very first thing we did was to provide very large, naturalistic enclosures with a wide assortment of enrichment to help the bears make use of their natural curiosity and stimulate them to remain active. Twice a day, keepers enter the enclosures to 'paint' honey onto trees and rocks and position water melons where the bears need to search for them. Bears love nothing more than honey!

"We provide them with enrichment to stimulate their natural instincts, coupled with a healthy nutritious diet and large spaces to roam and interact with other bears. This helps the bears recover from their traumatic past."

Kadambari Atri, Wildlife SOS

The rescued bears enjoy exploring the natural surroundings of the sanctuaries. This is enriching the lives of the bears and making every day interesting and unpredictable, as it is in the wild.

Searching for and then stretching or climbing to reach these succulent water melons helps to stimulate a bear's natural behaviour in the wild where finding food is rarely easy.

They deserve all the tasty treats we can give them.

Bears enjoying a 'wobble tree' enrichment. When they shake the 'tree' fruits and nuts cascade down onto them!

There's nothing the bears love more than licking honey.

Tasty watermelon frozen in ice blocks makes absorbing and refreshing enrichment for the bears in the heat of summer.

Coconut chunks and dollops of honey help to make for happy bears!

A handful of honey helps the medicine go down!

Kalandar Rehabilitation Project

For at least 400 years the Indian Sloth Bear (Melursus ursinus) has been exploited. Over the centuries a nomadic tribe known as the Kalandars used the bears as a means of generating an income for their families.

In 1996 it was thought there were more than a thousand dancing bears throughout India. Poachers would kill the adults and sell their cubs for around $7.50 each. The Kalandars would buy the cubs to use as dancing bears. Before he was even six months old, without using any anaesthesia, a red-hot poker would be forced through the baby bear's muzzle to make way for either a coarse rope or a metal ring which was destined to stay in his nose for the rest of his life. Worse was to come when the bear was a year old. To prevent the young bear from biting, his incisors and canine teeth would either be smashed to pieces or ripped out to be sold as lucky charms. No anaesthesia was used: it's impossible for us to imagine the pain the bears were left in from their broken teeth and infected gums.

Bears would accompany their owners over long distances looking for tourists who would pay to see a bear dance. It was a hard life for both the bear and its owner.

Sloth bears have been protected by law since the Wildlife Protection Act came into force in India in 1972. However, it wasn't until 2002, when a coalition of animal welfare groups came together, that the Agra Bear Rescue Facility was built and there was a place to house the rescued bears. Since then, more than 600 bears have been rescued and given a permanent, safe home to live out their lives free from fear and pain. There are now also bear rescue centres in Bannerghatta and Bhopal. There are no longer any dancing bears to be seen on the streets of India.

Treating the Kalandars with dignity and respect and compensating them for their only source of income was always going to be key to saving the bears. This policy proved to be a resounding success. One by one Kalandar tribespeople handed over their bears in return for modest compensation and a written commitment never to own or exploit a bear again. Many have now gone on to open their own businesses while others now work at the rescue centres.

Kalandar children are now able to attend school and receive an education sponsored by the Kalandar Rehabilitation Project, instead of following their parents into exploiting dancing bears. So far more than 1360 children have benefitted from this programme.

The Kalandars lacked all education and had been marginalised by society at large in India. The men who exploited the bears did so to put food on the table for their families by the only way they knew how. Once a bear had been handed over, the bear's owner was taught new skills to enable him to make a better living for himself and provide an education for his children.

"We realised early on that there was no point rescuing bears unless we also gave the Kalandars new skills that would enable them to earn a living without making bears dance."

Kartick Satyanarayan, co-founder, Wildlife SOS

Some of the Kalandars earn a living from making snacks...

...and delivering them to small roadside shops.

This Kalandar couple earn a living packaging up different spices for sale.

Cooking snacks for sale.

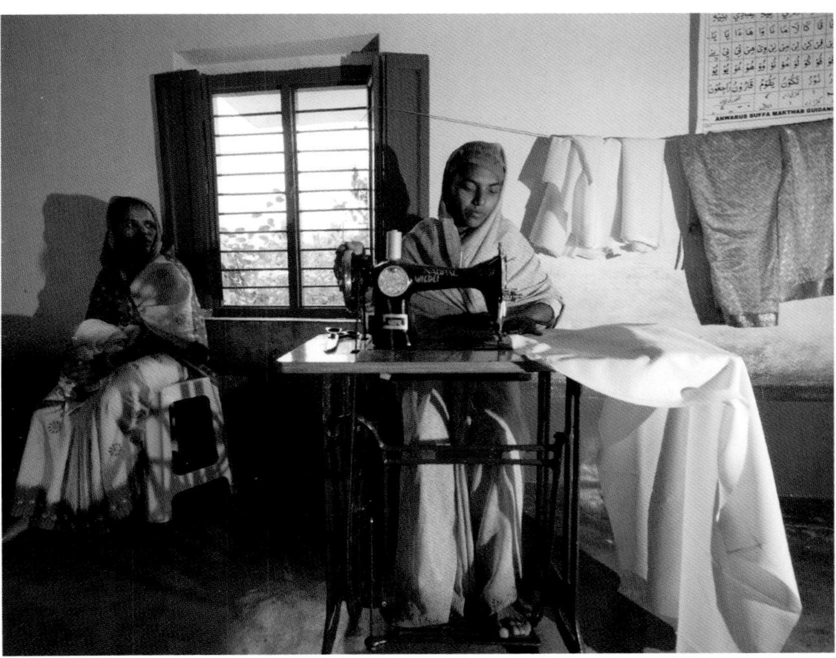

Kalandar women learn new skills such as sewing and embroidery, empowering them to earn their own wage and building their confidence and self-esteem.

Weaving is a popular vocation among the Kalandars.

"We give the Kalandars self-esteem and responsibility by teaching them different vocations so that they can stand up proudly in society."

Kartick Satyanarayan, Co-Founder of Wildlife SOS

"The organisation's Dancing Bear Rehabilitation Project was supported by the Ministry of Environment and Forests and the State Forest Department. They sponsored education and provided alternative livelihoods for the Kalandar communities who for centuries were dependent on sloth bears to earn a living."

Wildlife SOS

Some former bear handlers set up roadside stalls selling fruit and vegetables to earn a living.

Thankfully, with the passing of time, dancing bears have become part of history and the Kalandars are reaping the benefits of regular employment and schooling for their children.

"At Free the Bears we are overjoyed at the success of this project and are committed to ensuring that the bears are never again forced to dance on the streets of India. That sad chapter of animal welfare history has been closed forever. Happily, we have been able to transform the lives of both the bears and their handlers, thus ensuring a lasting solution for both animals and people."

Mary Hutton, Founder of Free the Bears Fund in Australia

Bhopal Bear Rescue Centre

Bhopal was the third of the bear rescue centres to be set up by our partners Wildlife SOS. It is situated in the centre of India in the state of Madhya Pradesh.

The city of Bhopal is infamous for the terrible disaster at the Union Carbide refinery back in December 1984 when a pesticide cloud leaked from the plant: 2000 people died immediately and 6000 have died since. Over 600,000 people were injured.

Bhopal is situated on a beautiful lake and the Van Vihar National park is on the southern shores of the lake. The bear sanctuary is housed within the National Park and it took bears from the local region of India. Twenty-seven bears live there within approximately 20 acres.

The entrance to the Vin Vihar sanctuary and bear rescue centre in Bhopal.

Preparing porridge for the bears in Bhopal.

To avoid any arguments over food each bear has its own bowl which also enables keepers to monitor each individual bear's food consumption.

A happy, healthy bear in Bhopal.

Enjoying just being a bear at the Bhopal rescue centre.

The bears at all our rescue centres have plenty of space and enrichment to keep them active and stimulated.

Children attending an education camp in Bhopal benefit from the Kalandar Rehabilitation Project, not least by receiving an education – something their parents missed out on.

Bannerghatta Bear Rescue Centre (BBRC)

At the end of 2005 International Animal Rescue and Wildlife SOS were given the chance to set up a second sanctuary for dancing bears in India within the beautiful Bannerghatta Safari Park outside Bangalore.

The nature reserve is home to antelope, elephants, tigers, crocodiles and a variety of wild birds, and at the centre of the forest is a 37-acre area set aside for bears. Twenty-six bears were being kept in cages in the park in appalling conditions. They were suffering terribly from their long imprisonment and showing signs of psychological and physical trauma.

The Indian Conservator of Forests was extremely concerned when he learned of the neglect of the bears. He contacted Wildlife SOS for advice and they in turn called on International Animal Rescue for help.

Once the Conservator of Forests had visited the Agra bear sanctuary, he knew International Animal Rescue and Wildlife SOS could be trusted to look after the bears in Bannerghatta. The two charities were given the go ahead to care for them and improve the conditions they were living in as well as convert their 'prison' into a brand-new sanctuary that could also accommodate other rescued bears in the south of India.

This was a major breakthrough in the campaign to rescue bears in India. It spelled an end to the misery of the 26 bears and also provided the foundations for the sanctuary in southern India that the charities had been looking for.

Since those early days, much money and time has been invested in Bannerghatta so that the care and housing it provides for the bears equal the standards in Agra.

Charities working together for the common good have saved hundreds of bears from a life of constant, excruciating pain and continual abuse.

L to R: two young members of the WSOS team caring for the bears; Dr Arun Sha, Chief Vet at BBRC; a supporter of Free the Bears with Mary Hutton, FTB Founder; Matt Hunt, CEO of FTB; WSOS team member; Gavin Bruce, Director of Operations at IAR; Geeta Seshamani, Co-Founder of WSOS; Alan Knight, CEO of IAR; two more young members of WSOS who care for the bears.

When he was brought into the BBRC, the nose of this poor bear was bloodied and torn by the ring forced through it.

Bannerghatta: another beautiful bear mutilated and scarred by a vicious nose piercing.

The last dancing bears in India arrive at the Bannerghatta Bear Rescue Centre.

A brand new rescue centre was built to accommodate the rescued bears.

L to R: Geeta Seshamani and Kartick Satyanarayan, Co-Founders of Wildlife SOS; Mary Hutton, Chief Executive of Free the Bears and Gavin Bruce, Operations Director at International Animal Rescue.

Feeding time at the Bannerghatta Bear Rescue Centre!

The bears are anticipating access to their quarters where a tasty meal of 'porridge' awaits them at the same time each day – and they uncannily know what the time is! The bears are not locked up at night and are free to roam at will in their extensive enclosures.

Bannerghatta bear laid back and loving life.

Spotlight on KAVYA

Kavya is one of the resident sloth bears at the Bannerghatta Bear Rescue Centre. Her life started on a tragic note. She was only a cub when poachers entered her forested home and snatched her away from her mother. She was later sold into the dancing bear trade in early 2007 and the following nine months of her life were filled with inconceivable pain and fear as she was made to go through a brutal indoctrination process that aimed to break her spirit.

Fortunately, our rescue team found Kavya in a small Kalandar settlement in Bellary district, Karnataka and brought her back to the centre. She was placed under mandatory quarantine so she could familiarise herself with her new home and receive necessary treatment. But it wasn't long before Kavya was introduced to other bears in the hope that she might make some new friends and start afresh. Socialisation plays a big role in the rehabilitation process and gives the bears a chance to hone their natural instincts and skills. We realised however that, unlike her fellow companions, Kavya was not very sociable. Even today, she mostly keeps to herself but on rare occasions we have seen her playing with two female bears - Dolly and Bharathi. We remain hopeful that this might someday blossom into a happy, long lasting friendship.

Kavya is quite active and spends most of her day playing with various structural enrichments in her enclosure, her favourite being the suspended fruit enrichments. She has a hearty appetite and enjoys gulping down her honey-laced porridge, which usually leaves its mark in the form of a porridge moustache! A satisfying lunch is never complete without a well-deserved nap and Kavya enjoys her afternoon siesta sprawled out in the hammock under the tree. Given her temperamental nature, she can be territorial at times and will charge at any bear that approaches her den or hammock.

Monsoon showers bring about a much-needed respite from the heat across India and Kavya seems to enjoy taking full advantage of the drop in temperature. She spends most of the day playing outside in the rain and digging up termite mounds around her enclosure.

Wildlife SOS

Kavya's favourite enrichments are the fruits (watermelon in this instance) which keepers place all round the large enclosures. Searching for food is the natural behaviour of sloth bears and this activity helps to keep them active, stimulated and healthy.

After working so hard to retrieve the tasty watermelon, a bear definitely deserves a well-earned nap!

Feeding the bears in Bannerghatta – and at the other rescue centres - is a serious and time consuming business. Every day at 4am the food preparation begins. The food consumption of every individual bear is monitored daily to ensure they do not become overweight and also to look out for any early signs of poor health; a bear that's not hungry at feeding time would be a cause for concern and further investigation.

WILDLIFE SOS
INDIA

BANNERGHATTA BEAR RESCUE CENTRE

BBRC DAILY ENCLOSURE WISE FEED DISTRIBUTION GUIDE

ENCLOSURE NAME	NUMBER OF CANS (PORRIDGE)	MILK (L)	BOILED VEGETABLES (APPROX.) (Kg)	BOILED EGGS (Numbers)	SEASONAL FRUITS (Kg)	HONEY (APPROX.) (Kg)
PANCHAVTHI (15 BEARS)	2 FULL (80 Kg)	2	5	30	38	1.5
CHITRAKUTA (15 BEARS)	2 FULL (80 Kg)	2	5	30	42	1.5
KISHKINDA (16 BEARS)	2 FULL (80 Kg)	2	5	26	35	1.5
DR.GKV (21 BEARS)	3 FULL (120 Kg)	2	8	42	65	2
JAMBHAVA (19 BEARS)	5 FULL & ½ BUCKET (115 Kg)	2	7	38	58	2

(UPDATED OCTOBER 2015)

Preparing a huge pot of 'porridge' for all the bears in Bannerghatta.

Porridge cooling off. Bears literally 'vacuum' up their meal making loud slurping noises in the process!

INGREDIENTS OF PORRIDGE

Barley, pearl millet, finger millet, grounded chick peas, dates, honey, eggs, jaggery (cane sugar), milk, sweet potato, carrot, pumpkin, bananas, turmeric, and salt. All cooked together with water and served twice a day to the bears. In the morning meal honey, eggs and dates are added to individual bear dishes. To the afternoon meal salt, jaggery, and bananas are added for extra taste.

Each bear consumes 4kg to 4.5 kg. In addition, at 12.30pm each day seasonal fruits are provided to the bears. After the last meal of porridge in the late afternoon peanuts, coconuts, roasted black chickpeas and puffed rice cakes are provided as a part of the enrichment programme. Bears are also able to search for termites and other insects in their vast and natural enclosures which they have access to day and night.

The Bear Repair Squad visits Bannerghatta

In May 2011 the charity brought a team of expert British vets, affectionately known as the Bear Repair Squad, to the Bannerghatta Bear Rescue Centre near Bangalore. Claudia Hartley, a leading veterinary eye specialist from the Animal Health Trust, and her colleagues Marian Matas Riera from Majorca and Claudia Busse from Germany were joined by anaesthesiologist Heather Bacon of the Royal School of Veterinary Studies at Edinburgh University.

A diet devoid of good nutrition, combined with the shocking abuse by their handlers, has left some bears blinded for life, while others have developed cataracts over the eyes. Lily was 13 years old and almost blind when rescued from a violent gang who had tortured her, leaving Lily in excruciating pain and almost blind.

Lily, soon to be pain-free and able to see clearly again having had cataracts removed, was in the safe and expert hands of the Bear Repair Squad.

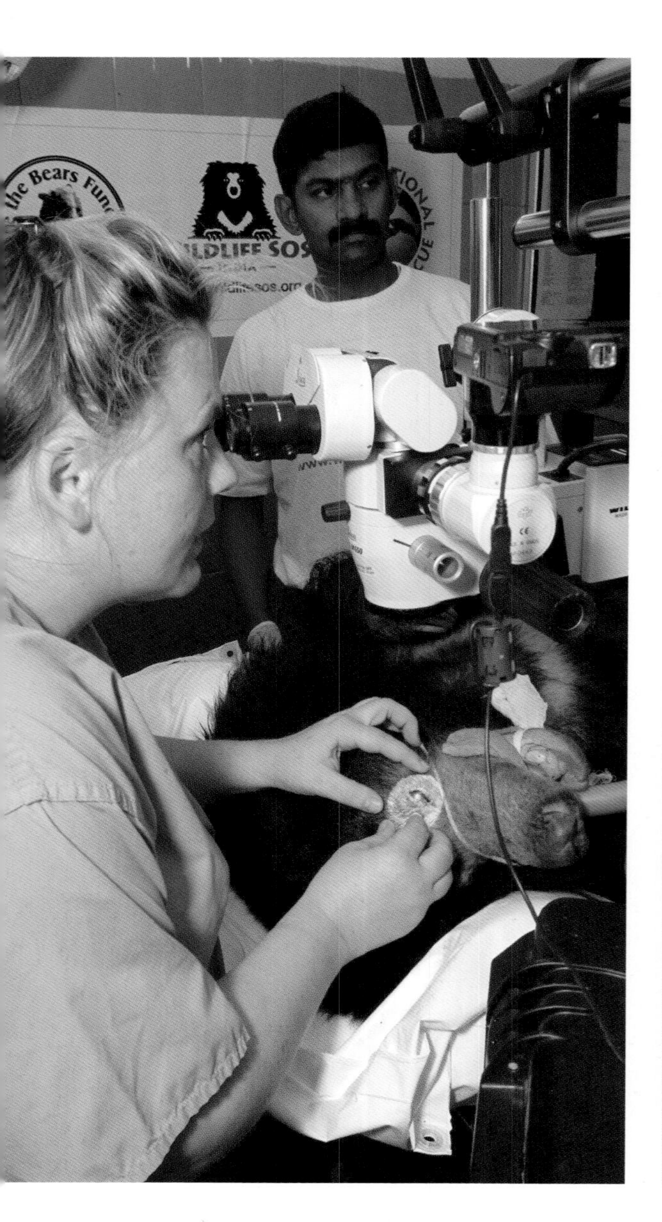

Claudia Hartley at work.

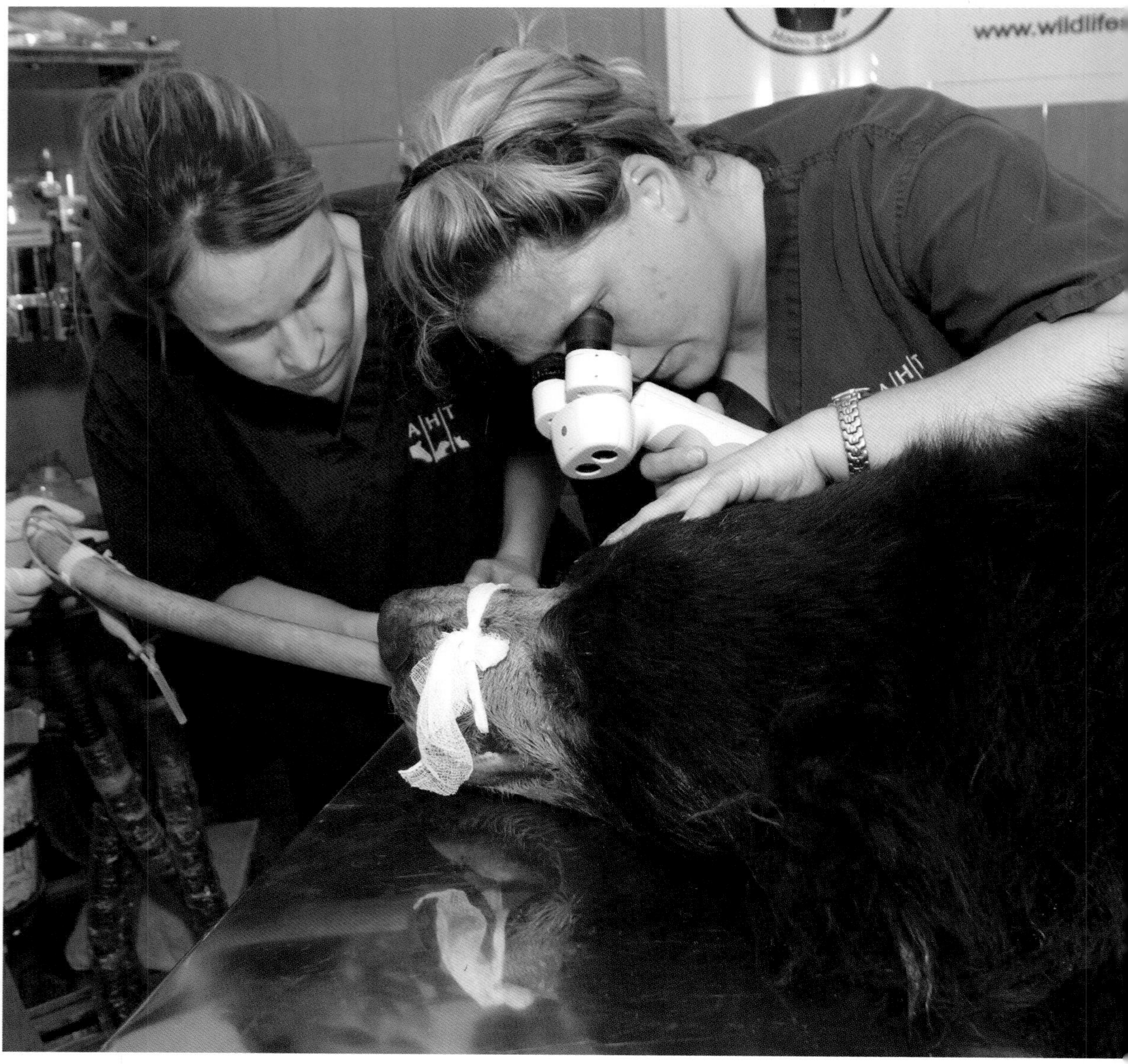

Claudia takes a close look at Lily's eye with the assistance of Marian Matas Riera.

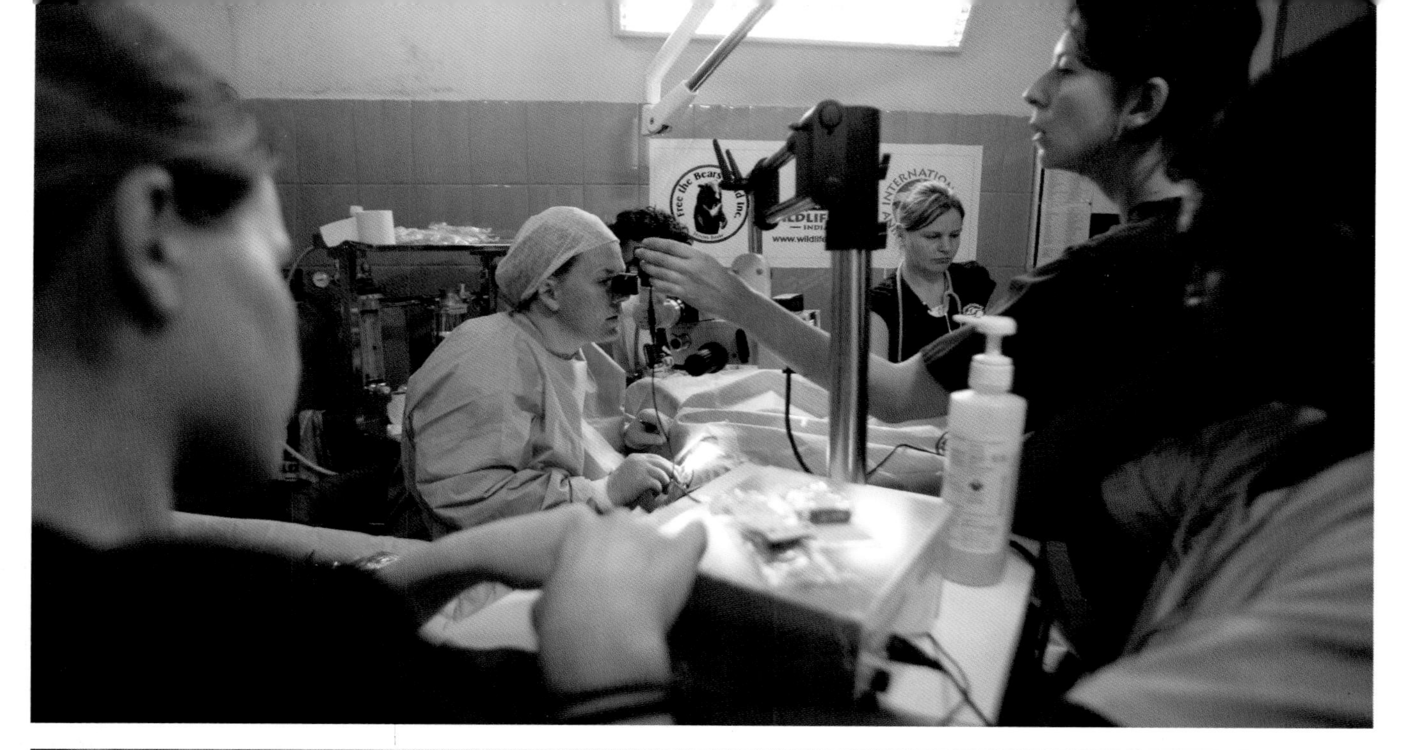

The Bear Repair Squad in action.

Free from pain and able to see clearly again, Lily wasted no time in making new friends.

Thanks to all the vets involved, the staff at the Bannerghatta Bear Rescue Centre, and the many generous supporters of IAR and Wildlife SOS, Lily is now a very happy, healthy bear, living with other bears in the 27-acre wildlife reserve managed by IAR's partners Wildlife SOS.

Spotlight on RATNA

Pleasant temperatures and lush green foliage are a normal occurrence during the year at the Bannerghatta Bear Rescue Centre (BBRC). Glittering pools of water are scattered throughout the centre, along with plenty of trees for the bears to clamber up. This world is drastically different from the one these bears once lived in, which was filled with pain and suffering. Ratna's initiation into this world was no different. For the first three years of her life, she had known nothing but torture as a dancing bear at the hands of her Kalandar master. We welcomed Ratna in to the BBRC family in 2009, and have since put in our best efforts to give her the life she truly deserves.

When Ratna arrived, she was predictably slow to trust and would be apprehensive of any keepers who were in her vicinity. However, slowly but surely the young bear was able to associate our staff with positive reinforcements. Now her favourite face to see is of her keeper, Jagath, who greets her enthusiastically every day!

Although these bears were given their name because they have long claws similar to sloths, Ratna has clearly interpreted it differently by adopting sloth-like behaviour. While most bears love to climb trees, run around their enclosure, and explore the various enrichments, Ratna is more inclined to fall asleep at times of excitement and fun. Consequently, she has been labelled BBRC's 'laziest bear'. The goofy bear has been observed accidentally somersaulting from her hammock while she is in the process of dozing off or already in a deep slumber. Her talents also include the ability to contort into silly positions while she sleeps, which often confuses the keepers when trying to distinguish her rear from her head!

When summer arrives, the bears receive a variety of different foods to eat. Ratna has developed quite a sweet tooth and enjoys eating as many watermelons as she can get her paws on, as well as honey, dates, and popcorn. Ratna looks forward to mealtimes, which are her favourite part of the day. Once satisfied with her meal, she heads over to the shade and proceeds to laze around and nap while she is digesting her food outside in the rain and digging up termite mounds around her enclosure.

Wildlife SOS

Ratna keeping an eye out for the arrival of her next meal!

Ratna – pretty as a picture.

Ratna caught on camera in a yoga pose!

With a fully belly it's time for a nap, sweet dreams Ratna!

Saddam once owned a bear but now is an enthusiastic and key member of the team at the Bannergatta rescue centre. Most days he prepares food enrichment to keep the bears occupied and healthy. While some food like this gourd is stuffed full of dates and honey and positioned so the bears have to climb to reach it, other fruits are hidden in trees or behind rocks.

"In 1972 the dancing bears in India were outlawed by Parliament under the Wildlife Protection Act. While a lot was done under the Act, the bears weren't touched because the zoos wouldn't take them and there were no shelters. There was simply nowhere to keep them. Thankfully Wildlife SOS stepped in and, with financial backing from International Animal Rescue, was able to build a sanctuary to house and care for the rescued dancing bears. On 24 December 2002 the Agra Bear Rescue Facility opened its doors to the first six bears to be taken off the streets. And the rest is history. Nowadays, dancing bears are no longer seen on the busy tourist routes in India: instead, they can be found living peacefully in cool, shady sanctuaries and the cruel practice of dancing bears has been consigned to the history books once and for all."

Maneka Gandhi,
Indian Union Cabinet Minister for Women & Child Development in the Government of PM Narendra Modi.
She is also an animal rights activist, environmentalist, and widow of the Indian politician Sanjay Gandhi.

West Bengal to Bannerghatta

In 2010 serious threats from Maoist insurgency groups in India led to the emergency evacuation of rescued dancing bears and staff from what was a fourth bear rescue centre, located in West Bengal. The facility, located in Purulia district, had been established by Wildlife SOS in collaboration with the West Bengal Government and Forest Department with support from International Animal Rescue and Free the Bears, Australia. It had been home to the bears ever since they had been rescued from their miserable lives on the streets of India.

"When the West Bengal Forest Department and the Rescue Centre received the warnings from the Maoist insurgency groups to evacuate all staff from the forest area, we were seriously concerned. We realised that they meant business and an emergency evacuation was of the utmost urgency," **said Kartick Satyanarayan, Co-founder of Wildlife SOS.**

"The Maoist groups pinned up a poster with the words "Leave the forest if you wish to remain safe." We immediately appealed to the Zoo Authority of Karnataka, the West Bengal Government and the Central Zoo Authority of the Government of India to facilitate the safe evacuation from the centre in the interests of the safety of people and animals."

Alan Knight, Chief Executive of International Animal Rescue.

The situation was of grave concern after several wild animals, birds and snakes had been burnt alive in a Maoist attack in December 2009 in Jhargram Zoo in West Bengal. The Bannerghatta Biological Park, Karnataka Forest Department, Zoo Authority of Karnataka, Central Zoo Authority and Wildlife SOS facilitated the safe evacuation of the 22 bears -12 males and 10 females. *"We are extremely grateful to Bannerghatta for making it possible for us to rescue these animals from a critically dangerous situation,"* **Kartick Satyanarayan added.**

The bears were fed and monitored at regular intervals on the long journey from West Bengal to their arrival at Bannerghatta, Bangalore.

They were evacuated with the help of three large trucks and a team of about 12 trained staff and a veterinarian travelled with the bears to ensure their safety and wellbeing.

From pain to paradise for the former dancing bears of India.

The rescued bears have everything they need to enjoy life – food, forest and plenty of freedom, as well as expert, loving care to keep them healthy and happy.

Spotlight on DURGHA

Durgha was rescued from Ramnagara and brought to Wildlife SOS in 2007 as a result of a human-wildlife conflict incident. At the time she was just a little five-month old cub and had already had a bad start in life, without her mother to nurture and care for her.

It has now been over 12 years since Durgha joined our bear family, and she is doing better than ever. Gone are the days of uncertainty for this bear, as she is busy living her life to the full at the Bannerghatta Bear Rescue Centre (BBRC). As time has progressed she has developed an eccentric personality. The team had begun to notice that she would occasionally go missing from her enclosure for a while. After much investigation the staff discovered that Durgha was living a double life. When she was not in her enclosure, she would be off exploring the centre. No one would ever have known if one of the keepers hadn't seen her wandering around! It was almost as if she was a rebellious teenager sneaking out of her bedroom to have an adventure.

Durgha shares her enclosure with three other bears by the name of Ankur, Megha and Dhoni. These four bears love each other's company and are often observed rolling around while play-wrestling, and chasing each other up in to the trees as a form of bear tag. If one bear is lounging in the hammock, it doesn't take long for Durgha to lumber over and roll off whoever is swinging in bliss! When she wants to spend quality time on her own, Durgha likes to dig holes around the enclosure and then emerges covered in dust from the tips of her ears to the points of her paws.

Back in March the vets noticed a change in Durgha's eating habits. After a few consultations with the veterinary team, it was clear that she had developed dental issues like many of the bears that are being rehabilitated at our centre. An x-ray examination showed that her right upper and her left lower canines were dead. After receiving a standard root treatment at the beginning of April, her condition showed improvement fairly quickly. Now, just like any happy bear, she loves to chomp on watermelon, honey, dates and porridge.

Wildlife SOS

Durgha the escape artist!

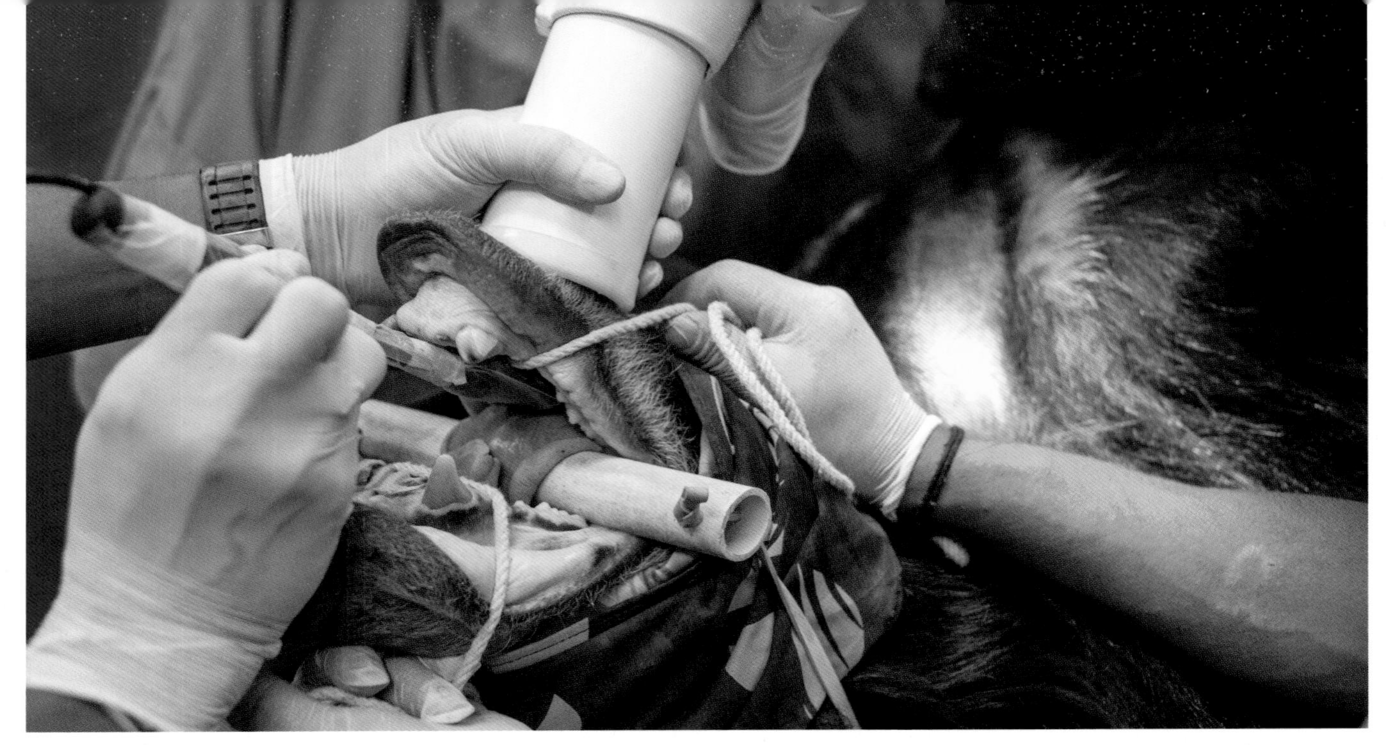

Durgha undergoing dental treatment.

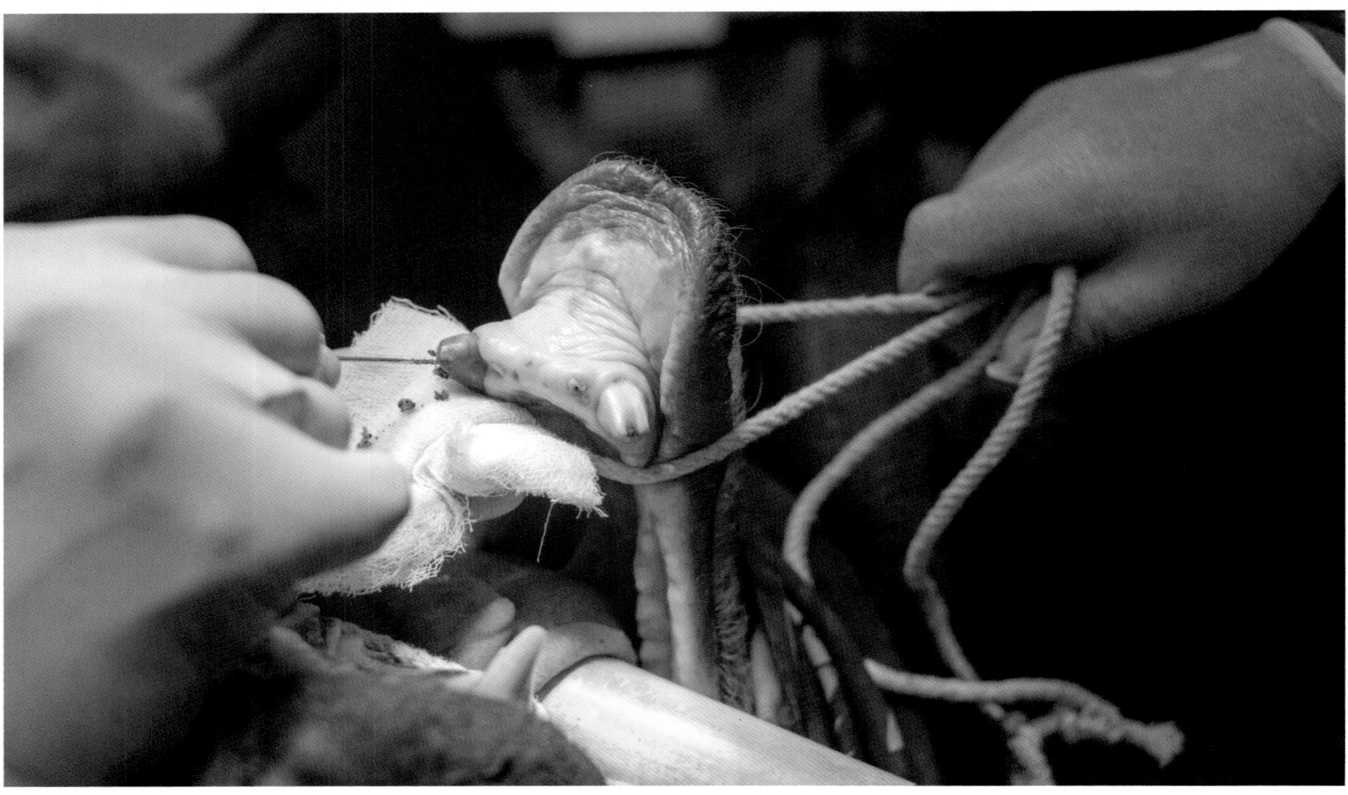

Durgha, pain free, tucking into her favourite fruit - watermelon.

Unwelcome visitors are a not uncommon occurrence at the Bannerghatta Rescue Centre. Staff are all trained to watch out for snakes and anti-snake-bite venom is kept in storage. Any snake found on the premises is caught and released in a nearby forest.

It's always rewarding to see the rescued bears looking so happy and contented.

Professionally managed with nothing left to chance.

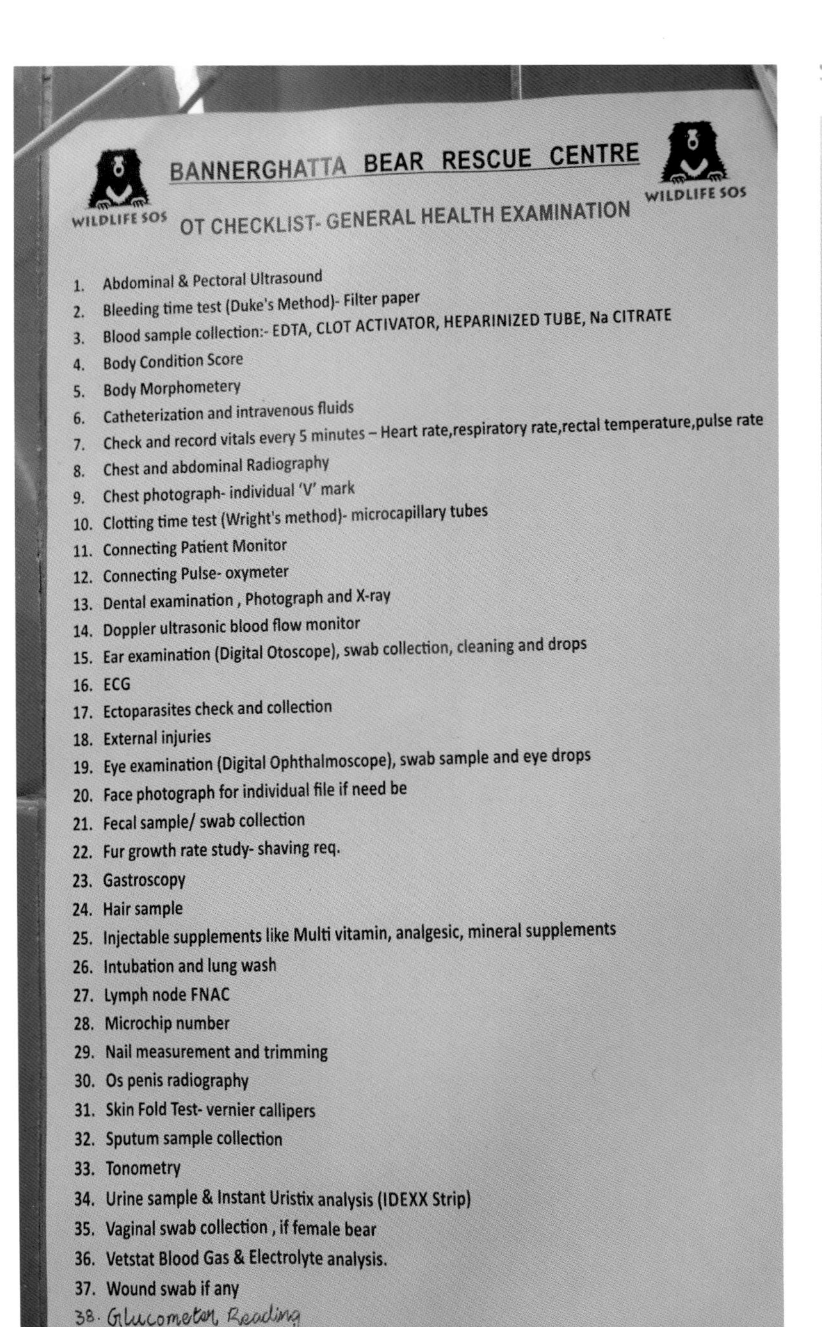

BANNERGHATTA BEAR RESCUE CENTRE

WILDLIFE SOS

OT CHECKLIST- GENERAL HEALTH EXAMINATION

1. Abdominal & Pectoral Ultrasound
2. Bleeding time test (Duke's Method)- Filter paper
3. Blood sample collection:- EDTA, CLOT ACTIVATOR, HEPARINIZED TUBE, Na CITRATE
4. Body Condition Score
5. Body Morphometery
6. Catheterization and intravenous fluids
7. Check and record vitals every 5 minutes – Heart rate,respiratory rate,rectal temperature,pulse rate
8. Chest and abdominal Radiography
9. Chest photograph- individual 'V' mark
10. Clotting time test (Wright's method)- microcapillary tubes
11. Connecting Patient Monitor
12. Connecting Pulse- oxymeter
13. Dental examination , Photograph and X-ray
14. Doppler ultrasonic blood flow monitor
15. Ear examination (Digital Otoscope), swab collection, cleaning and drops
16. ECG
17. Ectoparasites check and collection
18. External injuries
19. Eye examination (Digital Ophthalmoscope), swab sample and eye drops
20. Face photograph for individual file if need be
21. Fecal sample/ swab collection
22. Fur growth rate study- shaving req.
23. Gastroscopy
24. Hair sample
25. Injectable supplements like Multi vitamin, analgesic, mineral supplements
26. Intubation and lung wash
27. Lymph node FNAC
28. Microchip number
29. Nail measurement and trimming
30. Os penis radiography
31. Skin Fold Test- vernier callipers
32. Sputum sample collection
33. Tonometry
34. Urine sample & Instant Uristix analysis (IDEXX Strip)
35. Vaginal swab collection , if female bear
36. Vetstat Blood Gas & Electrolyte analysis.
37. Wound swab if any
38. Glucometer Reading

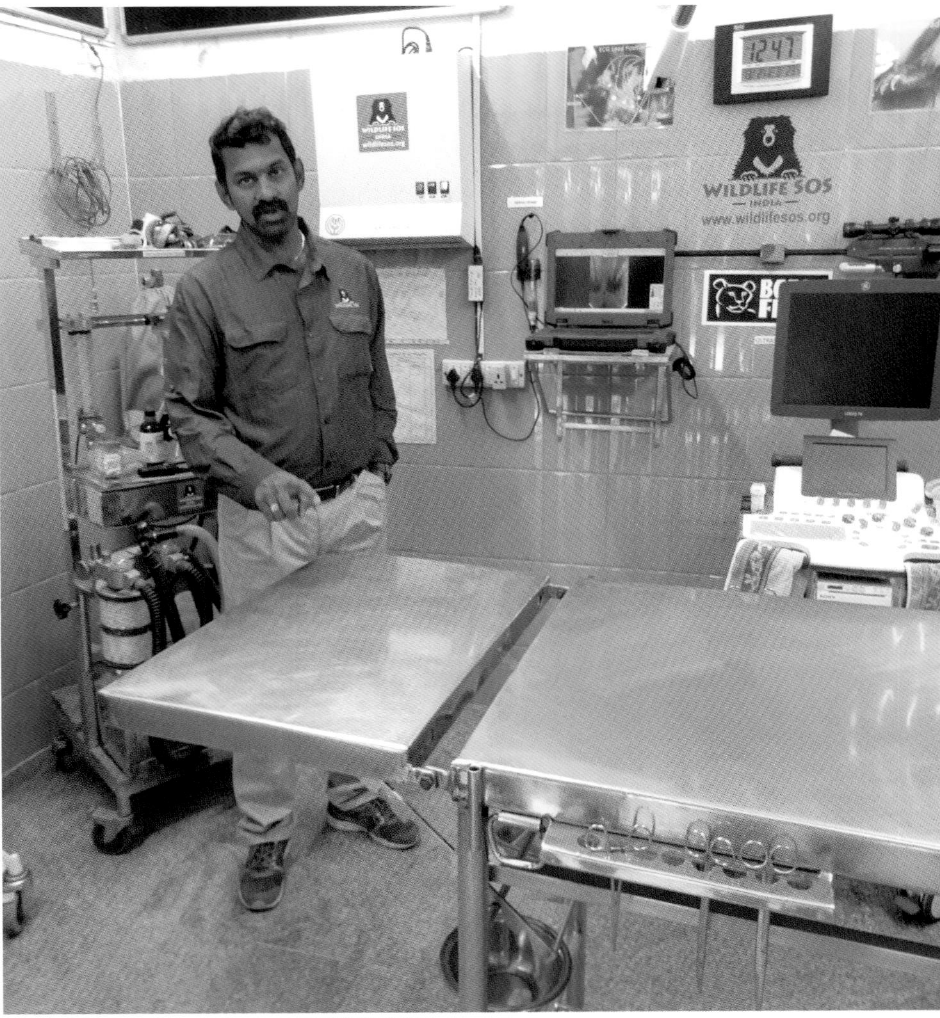

Once a year every bear is given a very detailed health check under the supervision of Dr Arun Sha, Wildlife SOS Director (Research and Veterinary Operations).

Spotlight on CHITRA

Chitra was the 500th bear we rescued, just before Christmas 2008. She gets her name from Chitradurga, the area in India where she lived her life as a dancing bear.

Chitra weighed a scrawny 62 kilos when she was first brought in to our Bannerghatta Bear Rescue Centre and she crouched in fear, expecting to be beaten. Her poor muzzle had been pierced several times, leaving it painfully swollen and inflamed and with a huge tear down one side. The ring through her delicate nose had to be surgically removed, along with the ropes wound tightly around her neck. Her canine teeth had been knocked out, leaving gaping, infected cavities in her gums.

Chitra has been with us for almost 12 years now and it has been truly heartening to watch her grow into the healthy, spirited bear that she is today! Life had clearly dealt Chitra an unfair hand and it was only natural for her to be conditioned into fearing and mistrusting humans. We had hoped Chitra would make some new friends at the centre because forming social bonds plays a vital role in the rehabilitation process. However, she has turned out to be surprisingly independent and even today she prefers to enjoy her own company!

Chitra is quite active and spends most of her day playing with various structural enrichments in her enclosure such as suspended fruit and tyres. True to her sloth bear instincts, Chitra is an expert at foraging and digging up insect mounds. She has taken to playing with hanging braid feeders that are stuffed with dates and honey. This has become her favourite post-breakfast ritual and she spends the better part of the day pulling out all the treats from feeder.

She has a feisty nature and can be quite headstrong, especially when it comes to listening to her keepers. But there is nothing that yummy treats can't solve and they work wonders for days when she is grumpy and needs a little pick-me-up. Chitra has emerged stronger and more beautiful from the dark, horrific conditions she was found in. Her story is one of hope and inspiration, and it makes us realise how worthwhile our efforts have been.

Wildlife SOS

Chitra taking a solitary stroll in the forest at the Bannerghatta Bear Rescue Centre.

Chitra is content with her own company.

The last dancing bear is rescued and animal welfare history is made

On 18th December 2009 the centuries-old tradition of dancing bears in India was finally brought to an end when Raju, the last remaining dancing bear, was surrendered at the gates of the Bannerghatta Bear Rescue Centre. This unforgettable day marked the end of a barbaric practice which had inflicted terrible cruelty on thousands of sloth bears. It was a momentous event in the history of animal welfare.

In just seven years, the coalition of International Animal Rescue (IAR), Wildlife SOS (WSOS) of India and Free the Bears Fund (FTB) Australia had rescued more than 600 bears from the streets and given them a safe, permanent home and lifelong, loving care in sanctuaries throughout India.

The project would not have succeeded without the rehabilitation package given to the Kalandar tribespeople when they handed over their bears. The Kalandar Rehabilitation Project enabled the bear handlers to learn new trades and find alternative, humane ways of earning a living and supporting their families.

For the first time Kalandar children were also able to attend school and receive an education, sponsored by the Kalandar Rehabilitation Project.

The entire project was – and continues to be - an unqualified success for both bears and conservationists.

It's 18th December 2009 and *Raju*, India's very last dancing bear, is being taken by his owner Raje Saab to the Bannerghatta Bear Rescue Centre. He was brought from over 100 kilometres away by truck.

"Today is a very memorable day for everyone involved in the dancing bear rescue project. Today we rescued Raju, the last dancing bear to walk the streets of India. He is not in great shape, undernourished and weighing less than 60 kg. But he will soon be healthy and enjoying his new life in the company of other rescued sloth bears at the centre."

Dr Arun Sha, Wildlife SOS Director (Research and Veterinary Operations)

While we all look at this and see the terrible cruelty involved, for Raje Saab making his bear 'dance' was the only way he knew how to provide food for his family. Like many other members of the Kalandar tribespeople, he was also following a tradition passed down over the centuries from generation to generation.

"Like most sloth bears who were subjected to this brutality, Raju's muzzle wound was never allowed to heal and his Kalandar master would tug on the rope to make him 'dance' and jump from the pain, to entertain the masses. To date we have rescued over 600 dancing bears. Our only objective is to give these animals the life of dignity and freedom they deserve."

Geeta Seshamani, Co-founder, Wildlife SOS.

Raje Saab is greeted by Alan Knight (IAR), Mary Hutton (Free the Bears), Geeta Seshamani and Kartick Satyanarayan (Wildlife SOS).

The official handover of *Raju* to the bear sanctuary required the completion of official documentation, including the payment of modest compensation for his owner's loss of income which would enable him to set up his own local business. This procedure had been conducted hundreds of times previously with great success, leaving a lasting goodwill between the bear rescuers and the Kalandar tribespeople.

The handover is completed with Raje Saab providing a thumbprint on the exchange of ownership document.

With the paperwork complete, Raje Saab receives a compensation cheque for handing over his bear. It would only be minutes before Raju was handed over to the rescue centre for a full health check and the start of a new life with other bears, free at last from pain and hunger.

It's time for Raje Saab to say goodbye and for *Raju* to make new friends, beginning with Alan Knight from International Animal Rescue.

Despite appearances, most of the Kalandars develop a very strong bond with their bears. Some handlers have even shown such understanding and empathy for the bears that they have gone on to be re-educated and employed in a variety of roles at the rescue centres.

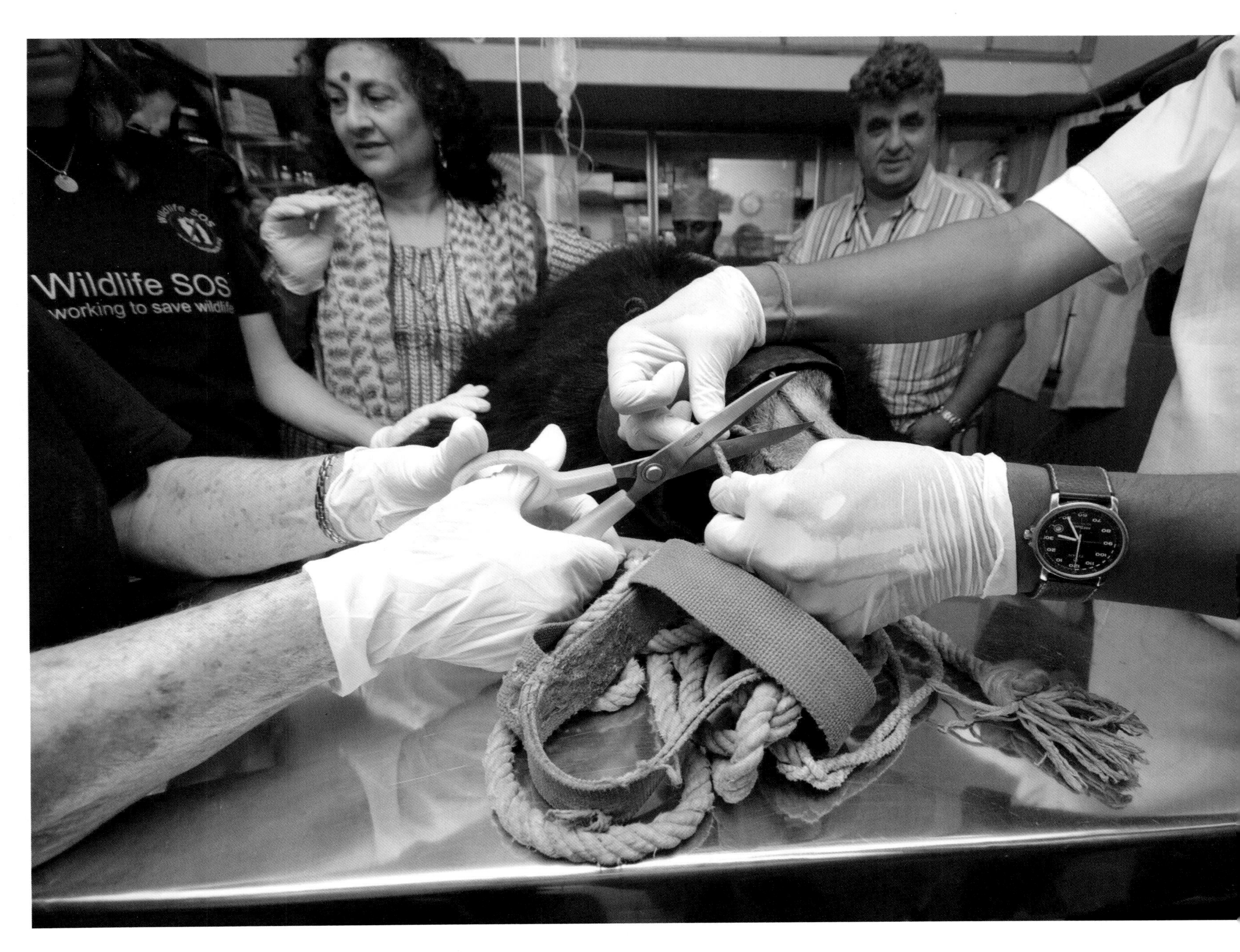

Safely in the arms of his rescuers, the most pressing issue is to remove the thick, coarse rope that was threaded through Raju's tender muzzle when he was less than a year old.

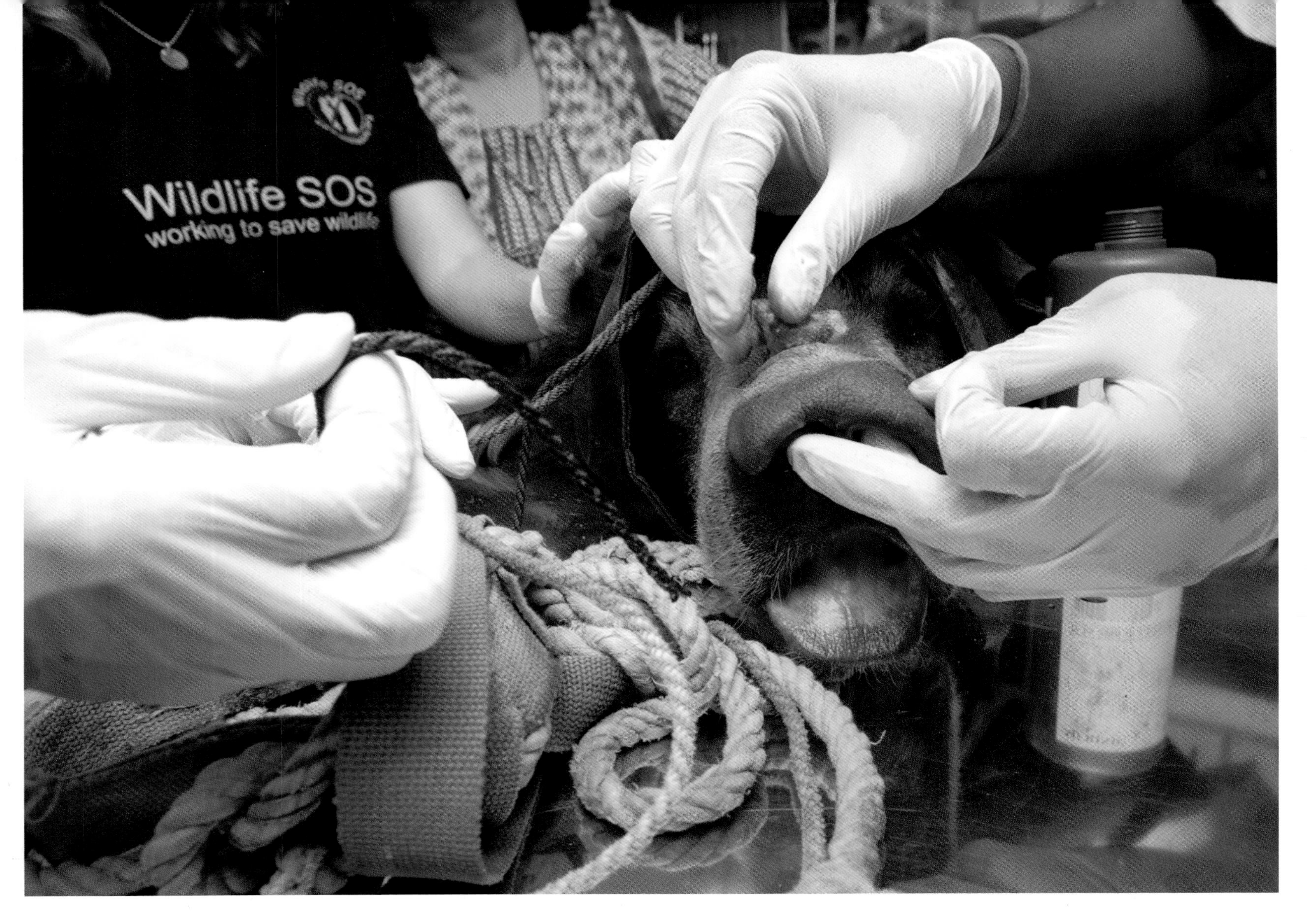

After eight agonisingly long and painful years, Raju is now free of the rope and the torment it caused him.

The rope through the nose was used by the owners to control the bears and make them 'dance' in the hope that people, particularly tourists, would pay money to watch what they thought was just an entertaining spectacle. But there was nothing entertaining about the way the rope was inserted into the bear's muzzle. First the bear cub would be held down by a group of men while an iron rod was heated over boiling hot coals. Then, without anaesthetic, the red-hot needle would be forced into the bear's nose and burn a hole through which the rope would be threaded. No pain-killing medication would be given afterwards and the wound was left open and usually became infected. To make the bear 'dance' the owner had only to tug on the rope and the tormented animal would rise up on its hind legs to try to escape from the pain.

"In all my years in animal welfare, I have never been part of such a resounding success story.

To transform the lives of hundreds of captive bears is amazing in itself. But to put an end to this cruelty once and for all is nothing short of momentous.

We have always been immensely proud to be part of this project which we will continue to support now that all the bears have been rescued. I would like to say a huge thank you to everyone who has helped us over the years: none of the groups involved could have been part of this incredible achievement without the generosity and kindness of their members and supporters."

Alan Knight OBE, Chief Executive, International Animal Rescue.

Free from pain and fear, Raju is able now to spend his days quietly and contentedly.

We can only wonder what Raju is thinking and hope he no longer remembers the horror of his life on the streets.

Time for a nap!

A happy ending for all

Rani was brought in weighing 40 kilograms. She is now a thumping 120 kilograms owing to the nutritious food she has been getting from the cook, 31- year-old Manoj Kalandar, who has to endure the furnace-like intensity of the open fires in the kitchen where the meals are prepared in huge cauldrons.

Manoj got the cook's job in 2007 after his father surrendered his bear, Rosie, in return for 50,000 rupees ($870) as part of Wildlife SOS's rehabilitation package. Manoj says the income from Rosie's dancing used to support his 10 siblings.

When he was a young boy Manoj tended Rosie. In one way, the bear was a member of the family, living, eating and sleeping near them. In another, she was ruthlessly exploited.

"My father used to buy cubs from Assam and spend six months training them. We travelled all over, on the roads, outside hotels, making Rosie dance. Each dance lasted about 15 minutes," he says.

With their nomadic existence over, Manoj's son and daughter attend a local school. His wife has learnt sewing through the Kalandar Rehabilitation Programme, which aims to give sustainable alternative livelihoods to former dancing bear masters and their families so that they never return to keeping dancing bears to earn a living. Indeed, over time whole villages have relinquished their bears.

By abandoning bear dancing, the former owners are much better off. Their salaries in the shelters may be modest but Kartick Satyanarayan of Wildlife SOS points out that their income from bears used to be seasonal, depending on tourism, whereas now their incomes are more stable.

"In the months when they didn't earn from bears because there were no tourists, they used to beg. Now they live stable lives, their kids go to school and they enjoy a better quality of life," he says.

The Last Dance is Over

After 400-500 years the tradition of capturing bear cubs and torturing them into submission is over.

No more starvation, no more red-hot irons through their noses, no more excruciating pain from infections, no more claws pulled out with pliers, no more beatings, no more 'dancing' on the streets.

It's over. Consigned now to the history books.

None of this could have been achieved without donations from supporters of the various organisations involved.
Please accept our most sincere thanks for being there for the bears and responding generously when we asked for your help.

Saving India's Dancing Bears has always been a team effort

Mary Hutton of Free the Bears, Geeta Seshamani of Wildlife SOS, Alan Knight of International Animal Rescue and Kartick Satyanarayan of Wildlife SOS with the team at the Bannerghatta Bear Rescue Centre on the day of the rescue of Raju, the last dancing bear. Raju's handler, Raje Saab, is on the right at the back.

International Animal Rescue (IAR)

International Animal Rescue's mission is not only to save animals from suffering but also to rehabilitate and release them back into the wild and protect their precious natural habitats. IAR's work includes cutting free and caring for captive bears in India and Armenia, rescuing and rehabilitating orangutans and other primates in Indonesia and treating injured and orphaned howler monkeys in Costa Rica. The charity aims to return animals to their natural environment wherever possible, but also provides a permanent home for those that can no longer fend for themselves.

As human populations expand, wildlife comes under increasing threat. By rescuing critically endangered animals like the orangutan and reintroducing them into protected areas in the wild, IAR's work also plays a role in the conservation of threatened species.

International Animal Rescue works to educate the public in the compassionate and humane treatment of all animals and the need to protect and preserve their natural environment. IAR seeks always to find practical solutions that will benefit both animals and people.

www.internationalanimalrescue.org